FIELD GUIDE
to
Hallmarks
of
US Military Insignia

www.1903.com
Joe Weingarten

To my Grandchildren who hopefully will never see war

Oliva
Grant
Grace
Noah
Chole
Ben
Elise

and to those men and women who did not come home.

ISBN-13:978-1519118882
ISBN-10:1519118880

Copyright 2015 by Joseph L. Weingaren

This book contains material protected under International and United States Copyright Laws and Treaties. Any unauthorized reprint or use of this material is prohibited. No part of this book may be reproduced or transmitted in any form or by any means, electronic or mechanical, including photocopying, recording, or by any information storage and retrieval system without express written permission from the publisher.

Published by 1903 press, www.1903.com
Fishers, Indiana
United States of America

Field Guide to US Military Insignia Hallmarks

Contents

Preface	v
History of Hallmarks	1
Dating US Insignia	3
Vintage Jewelry ID by pin findings	4
Insignia Pin Backs & Clutches	5
1920's- 1930's Clutches	6
World War II to Current Clutches	7
Metal Quality Marks	11
Other Silver Hallmarks by County / Region	13
US Military Hallmarks	15
Military Hallmark Coding	15
USMC Quartermaster Certification	17
Institute of Heraldry List of Concerns Authorized to Manufacturer Military Insignia.	18
Hallmarks (Actual and Historical A through Z)	28
Appendix A Jewelry Patents	224
Appendix B WWII German Manufacturers	227
Appendix C WWII German RMZ Numbers	229
Belt Buckle Manufacturers	231
Belt Buckles Without an RZM Number	233
Appendix D US Manufacturers since 1965	235
Index	241

Preface

The initial concept of hallmarks was to prevent cheating in the manufacturing of jewelry and started in France in 1260-1275. It was an insurance that the maker stood behind what he made and the purity of the metal he used. Hallmarks as related to precious metals was codify in the United States in 1905. But much earlier in other countries.

This book is intended to provide a short history on hallmarks and metal purity but the primary focus is to be a quick guide to the many hallmarks used on military insignia to help in identification of who made the insignia and in some cases when. Also in some cases the names of manufacturers that did not have a hallmark or were contact suppliers to mainstream companies or just parts (called findings) suppliers.

This is part of a series of references guides to assist the collector and to correct many of the errors on web sites. The first in the series is a guide on US Paratrooper Badges.

This guide will show some of the insignia but more importantly the hallmarks and where possible a brief history of the hallmark owner. One of the problems is that many companies never registered their hallmarks with the US Patent Office but rather made one up and starting using it. The Gold and Silver Stamp Act of 1905 required a mark as to metal content if gold or silver and many companies added their name. WWII saw a change where even companies that were using their hallmark stopped when they sold items to the US Government. The government required that these not be marked to prevent the perception that they favored one supplier over another. Yet an exception to this rule existed when an item was sold via a base or fleet exchange or a private concern such as a uniform shop. This changed again in 1950 with a system started by the USMC Quartermaster that lasted only a few years and in 1953-54 with the introduction of the US Army's Institute of Heraldry numbering system. Where known the IOH assigned number are shown for each listing.

Will this guide ever be complete, I doubt it as time goes on new old hallmarks will be found, as will more information on companies. You will find many areas where I state no information is known. Be a hero and if you have a picture or information sent it to me at mrmac@aol.com. For example, after this book was submitted for proof, the IOH provide a new comprehensive list of all manufacturers with Numbers since 1965. So the names and some detail were added but we may be missing information.

Layout, all companies are listed in alphabetical order but even here this can be a problem. Where do you list Charles Polk Co. Under Charles or under Polk. I will use last names when this occurs. An index is provide so you can scan and find companies. In many cases some examples of insignia or medals are shown.

Special thanks to the following groups and individuals for their assistance in the development of this book: Dr. Howard G. Lanham, Dan Del Monico, Andrew H. Lipps, Thomas Casciaro, IOH, and Jim McDuff, ASMIC.

Joe Weingarten
Fishers, IN

Hallmarking

MD PS = "Pure Silver" from Mediolanum

Hallmarking is believed to have been started to insure the value of a coin. Only later did it come into being for jewelry starting in France in 1275 and later for insignia. As in some cases insignia was made by jewelry manufactures and they followed the law for medal content.

Official Roman coins from about the 4th century onwards show clear mint-marks indicating the city where the coin was minted, also often the officiant (workshop) that minted the coin and in the case of this coin that it is made of pure silver.

History

Webster defines a Hallmark as "the official mark stamped on gold and silver articles at Goldsmith's Hall in London as a guarantee of genuineness; hence, any mark or symbol of genuineness or high quality."

This is a very limited view considering hallmarks are also used to identify the manufacturer of the item and this was a requirement as far back as 1355. In viewing a hallmark we can say it is a distinctive mark mainly on precious metals to show who is the manufacturer and the quality of the metal. Today within the military it is no longer is used to show quality of the metal but rather the manufacturer.

Modern hallmarking in Europe appeared first in France, with the Goldsmiths Statute of 1260.

In 1275, King Philip III prescribed by royal decree, the mark for use on silver works.
In 1300 King Edward I of England enacted a statute requiring that all silver articles must meet the sterling silver standard (92.5% pure silver).

In 1313, his successor, Philippe IV "the Fair" expanded the use of hallmarks to gold works.

In 1355, individual maker marks were introduced in France, which was later mirrored in England in 1363, adding accountability to the two systems.

In 1424, the French Archbishop Jean de Brogny, after having consulted with a council of eight Masters Goldsmiths from Geneva, enacted a regulation on the purity and hallmarking of silver objects following the French standards for application in Geneva.

In 1427, the date letter system was established in France, allowing the accurate dating of any hallmarked piece.

In 1478, the Assay Office was established in Goldsmiths' Hall. At this time, the date letter system was introduced in England.

In 1697, a higher standard of silver, known as the Britannia standard (95.8% silver) was made compulsory in Great Britain to protect the new coinage which was being melted down by silversmiths for the silver. The Sterling standard was restored in 1720.

In 1851 Tiffany became the first US Company to introduce the English .925 sterling silver as a standard for their goods. In 1905 the United States adopted the National Gold and Silver

Stamp Act that set the standards within the USA and for items imported into the US.

Prior to 1950 the United States Military did not have a unified marking system. In the early 1950's time frame the USMC Quartermaster started a numbering system to keep track of insignia and who made the item with a 3 digit code which was called a serial number but actually was a certification number. One two digit code existed and was awarded to N.S. Meyer.

Every thing change in 1953-1954 when the US Army started a large effort to number all insignia purchased for both the Army and Air Force with the introduction of a identification system of a number followed by a single or double number. Then in 1965 the system now in use came into being where the number system changed and the system became a letter followed by a two digit number. For example the number assigned to the author was W32. With the letter in most cases representing the name the of the company. The Navy also adopted the IOH system and where a company had an IOH number when an item was made for the Navy they added a N to the hallmark. Also a block of numbers were awarded to the Navy for use to assign to their manufactures.

Dating US Insignia

No exact system exists on dating US insignia the following is an approximation of how to determine the date something was made.

Prior to 1905 - some items were marked based on European systems

1905 - National Gold and Silver Act (also called Stamp Act) required the marking of any item with precious metals. This Act is still the law of the land. So any item made in USA or imported for sale would be marked. It took a number of years for this to take hold.

WWII - Items manufacturer under US Military Contract did not to have the manufacturers name on the item, just metal content if required by the Stamp Act. Continued until early 1950's.

1950's - Items with a 3 digit number used by the Marine Corp Quartermaster in many cases they were called a serial number. But rather were a manufacturer ID number. These are part of the USMC Quality Assurance Certification Program (TM 10120-15/2)

1950's - Items marked GI were a certification mark by the military used during the Korean War era.

1953-54 to 1965 - A one or two digit number followed by a letter. Examples 1C or 14C. Most were a single digit only a few two digit codes existed.

1964 to 1974 - These were years that silver-filled was used on military insignia.

1965 to current - a single letter followed by two digits. Example W32, if am item was approved for Naval use an N would follow, example V21N. Sometimes it would be shown as V-21-N but the correct designation is without hyphens.

Vintage Jewelry ID by Pin Findings

http://www.fancy4glass.ca/information-gallery-main-pages/identifying-and-dating-an-antique-or-vintage-jewelry-clasp-or-hinge.htm

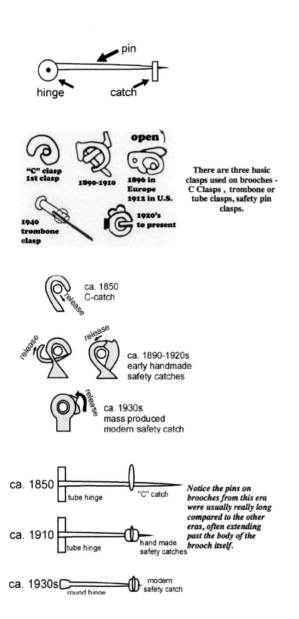

Insignia Pin Backs & Clutches

Without any question the best reference to the date on the use of post backs is by Dr. Howard G. Lanham and posted on the Internet at the following link. The information below is a summary of his excellent work and shown here with his permission.
http://hglanham.tripod.com/metalinsignia2/datingclutches.html

Prior to 1890's. The most common form or attachment for metallic insignia were attached by wire prongs or loops.

1890's. The first time screw backs became common as did pin backs with a simple metal C holder. The concept of the C holder was that the fabric would push the pin against the holder and prevent it from opening.

Screw back   C Holder

World War One and 1920's. The problem with the screw backs was the large hole they left on the uniform, so the pin back became the primary attachment for most insignia. A few high end companies started to use safety clasps such as what is commonly called the Tiffany clasp. Also towards the end of the war the center clap came into use on higher end items such as pilot wings.

Tiffany Safety Clasp   WWI Center Clasps   Modern

During the 1920's and 1930's companies refined the attachment of both jewelry and insignia. The common side opening C clasp came into being as did the clutch backs. The pin backs also had different styles and no common thread existed. The concept that a 30 or 40 or 80 degree opening pin would relate to a specific time period or thickness of the pin is false. Some pin backs were made with a rivet installed and some with a loop that was held in place by a V joint with protrusion that when pressed together held the pin in place.

1930's to today C clasp

V joint, pin with rivet

Loop pin with pressure V joint

This pin has a shoulder, the size of the shoulder is what resulted in a pin not fully opening. These are still made.

1920's- 1930's Clutches

Prior to WWII the use of clutch backs was very limited. The government procurement system required pin back or screw back. Only private purchased items came with clutch backs. Mainly officer insignia.

The Phinney clutch is considered the first one made for insignia and was invented by Elisha A Phinney and he applied for a patent on September 16, 1921.

On August 2, 1921, Charles Mendler of San Francisco patented another style clutch and received patent number 1,413,480 on April 11, 1922. But these clasps have not been seen on military insignia.

Another early clutch back came from AMCRAFT. It appears AMCRAFT tried various designs to develop a better clutch back.

Early Amcraft Type Clutches with a Squared Front

Back of same marked PAT AMCRAFT PENDING

Side View of an Early Amcraft Clutch

Stirrup Type Amcraft Top View
Rather than pulled by a disk this unusual type has a metallic stirrup.

Stirrup Type Amcraft Side View
This shows the metal stirrup.

Stirrup Type Amcraft Angled Side View
Better Showing the Stirrup

Late Amcraft Semiplastic Front View
This looks the same both kinds.

Late Amcraft Semiplastic Nonperforated Back View

Late Amcraft Semiplastic Perforated Back View

Late Amcraft Semiplastic Perforated Side View

World War II

As the story goes if a wing/insignia has a clutch back it is post WWII, but this is not true. Late war wings could have clutch backs and at the same time pin backs were used in both the 50's and early 60's. Rumor has it that in 1943 or 1944 the government started to ask for clutch back insignia, but the manufacturers claimed they had ample stocks of pin backs and wanted to use them up. According to the rumor the real reason was the need to purchase new equipment to install the pin on the insignia which at that time would cost about $25,000. a large sum and would take years for pay back. To get a better feel, look to Josten that used clutch backs during the war. One primary example is the WASP wing which was presented to the graduation of Class 44-1 on February 11, 1944. However they were ordered early and arrived late for the Class 43-8, December 17, 1943. Which would mean that Josten started using them on wings in late 1943. Both the Josten Senior and Command Pilot were only made in clutch backs.

The B. A. Ballou Company of East Providence, Rhode Island began producing clutches in 1942, having applied for its patent on May 13, 1942. It received patent number 2,308,412 for a securing device on January 12, 1943 with Frederick A. Ballou, Jr. and Melvin Moore being listed as the inventors. During the war they produced 300 million clutch backs. The first clutch backs were brass but were produced in both brass and silver, due to limits on brass as a war material needed for ammo. Here is a chronology of the Ballou clasps. Please note dates are approximate and based on patent applications and catalog listings.

Year	Type	Manufacturer	Marking	Image	Notes
1942	Plain	Ballou	Patent Pending *		brass 12.5mm
1942	Plain	Ballou	Patent Pending Sterling *		silver 12.5mm
1943	Plain	Ballou	Pat Nos 2308412 2308424		brass 12.5mm
1943	Plain	Ballou	Pat Nos 2308412 2308424		silver colored 12.5mm
1943	Plain	Ballou	Sterling Pat Nos 2308412 2308424		silver colored 12.5mm (Courtesy: Fred G. Rush, 3rd)
c 1945	4 Cleats	Ballou	Pat Nos 2308412 2308424 B in Star		silvered colored 10mm
c 1947	8 Cleats	Ballou	Pat Nos 2308412 2308424 B in Star		brass 12.5mm
c 1947	8 Cleats	Ballou	Pat Nos 2308412 2308424 B in Star		silver colored 12.5mm (Courtesy: Pieter Oosterman)

Year	Cleats	Maker	Patent/Mark	Image	Description
1948	8 Cleats	Ballou	Pat Nos 2308412 2308424		brass 12.5mm
1948	8 Cleats	Ballou	Pat Nos 2308412 2308424		silver colored 12.5mm
1951	8 Cleats	Ballou	Pat Nos 2308412 2308424 2551196		brass 12.5mm
Unknown	Plain	Unknown	None		brass 12.5mm generic post-patent or early prototype?
Unknown	4 Cleats	Unknown	None		brass 12.5mm
Unknown	4 Cleats	Unknown	None		brass 12.5mm (Courtesy: Pieter Oosterman)
after 1955	8 Cleats	Ballou	Ballou Reg'd		brass 12.5mm
after 1955	8 Cleats	Ballou	B.A.B. Reg'd		brass 12.5mm (Courtesy: Pieter Oosterman)
after 1955	8 cleats	Unknown	Improved Clutch		brass 12.5mm
after 1955	8 cleats	Unknown	Improved Clutch Japan		brass 12.5mm Imported by Denmark Military Co., NY
after 1955	8 cleats	Unknown	Hermes		brass 12.5mm (Courtesy: Pieter Oosterman)
after 1955	8 cleats	Unknown	None		brass 12.5mm
c 1960s	8 Cleats	Unknown	Made in USA		brass 12.5mm
c 1960s	8 Cleats	G.T. Jandy	Jandy Reg		brass 12.5mm

c 1960s-1996	8 Cleats	Unknown	Hermes		brass 12.5mm
c 1970s-1996	8 Cleats	His Lordship's Products	Lordship N.Y.		brass 12.5mm
c 1970s	8 Cleats	Ira Green, Inc	Ira-Green, Inc.		brass 12.5mm
c 1970s	8 Cleats	Unknown	Metal City		brass 12.5mm
c 1970s	8 Cleats	N. S. Meyer, NY	N.S. Meyer		brass 12.5mm
c 1970s	8 cleats	Unknown	None		brass 12.5mm
c 2000	8 Cleats	Ballou	Ballou Reg't 130 years		brass 12.5mm

A second, less common clutch type found on some World War Two era insignia are Tinnerman clutches. These were invented by Albert H. Tinnerman (1879-1961), whose company made all kinds of spring steel fasteners for industrial applications. Some of the newer Tinnerman clutches are marked with individual numbers and have a silver finish.

A third, even less common clutch type found on some World War Two era insignia are Rex clutches. The inventor of the Rex clutch was Frank Winters, who assigned his invention to the Rex Products Corporation of New Rochelle, N.Y. The patent was applied for on December 18, 1942 but not granted until April 3, 1945 as patent number 2,372,922. Examples of the clutches are marked "Patent Pending Rex."

Rex Clutch marked Patent Pending Rex   Rex Clutch Side View   Rex Clutch

A fourth WWII clutch back is called by Dr. Lamham a Ball Type. They are only marked patent pending and appear on armored collar insignia made by AMCRAFT.

"Ball Type" Clutches marked Patent Pending   "Ball Type" Side View

Post War - Assman clutches. They had were distinctive clutch backs that appear to look like the original Phinney's but hallmarked with their name. A flat backed C clasp was used in post war Germany on US insignia repaired and made in country.

Assmann Clutch marked with Assmann hallmark and AHA D.B.P.o.   Assmann Clutch Three-Quarter View

Current era. The patents on the Ballou clutch back ran out years ago, so many companies make these, especially overseas in China. The Ballou company went bankrupt in 2009 and was bought out by WR Cobb Co. They still produce the Ballou clasp. They also make a higher end clutch back called a "top hat" and a tie tack back.

Vietnam - during the Vietnam era a new plastic back started to show up in the far east. A couple of version existed in different colors as shown here. These are still in use as a low cost clasp.

Appendix A has several patents of clasps.

Metal Quality Marks

These are hallmarks that define the metal content of the product and do not have a relationship to any one manufacturer. The terms below are general and not specific to any one product. For example in the case of gold I have shown one quality (14 karat) but you can change the number to 14 or 18 and it would follow the same general rules.

In the United States all products that contain precious metals must be marked in accordance with the National Gold and Silver Stamp Act of 1905. Under this Act stiff fines were adopted to prevent mis-markings A $5000 fine per item that was sold and not marked or even properly advertised. For example selling something as Sterling when it was not Sterling the seller is subject to the fine with the money going to the buyer. But even before this Act a few terms started to pop up related to gold and silver. One such term was Acid Test - This was way to test for gold. So if an item is marked acid test it means it was tested for gold. This started as a simple test in the gold rush. When you put a drop of acid on gold nothing happens but it boils on base metals. So this was a simple test to prevent fools gold from tricking the buyer.

Before the California gold rush, the term acid test was used to say something met the acid test of time and can be found in early newspapers. So it withstood acid that burns even through metal. The product held up and was a sign of quality.

In WWII items were marked "ACID TEST" on the back, as s a hallmark of the quality. WW2 insignia manufacturers of the 1940's would hallmark this on plated items to show that the plating would stand the test of time and not wear off.

Silver:
Pure Silver: Fine Silver, .999, .999 Fine

Sterling Silver these marks are generally used: STERLING, STER, 925, STR, Sterling Silver (Sterling is 92.5% pure silver, 7.5% copper)

US Coin Silver two marks: COIN SILVER, 900 (90% pure silver, 10% other metals)

European Coin Silver: 800 (80% pure silver, 20% other metals)

Russian silver: 84, 88, 91 (this number is % of pure silver with the rest alloy)

Silver Filled - is marked to show, by weight, an amount of a silver layer on the outside of base metal. For example, the mark 1/10 Sterling. This means sterling silver layer is on the brass layer and is 1/10 the weight of the total metal in the item. 1/20 sterling would likewise mean the silver layer is sterling and it is 1/20 the weight of the total metal in the item.

Rolled Silver - Basically the same as silver filled. A very thin sheet of silver is rolled under a great deal of force on top of a base metal.

Silver Plate - a very thing electroplate layer of pure silver over a base metal. Sometimes some one will say an item is sterling plated which is impossible. Only fine silver can be plated onto another metal.

Nickel Silver / German Silver / is an alloy of 60% copper, 20% nickel and 20% zinc and contains no silver. It is also called nickel silver due to the color of the metal. It was developed in China during the Qing Dynasty.

Gold - 24Karat (24K, 24KP, .999) is pure gold and usually only found in coins or bullion bars. Lower levels of gold purity is achieved by mixing in various alloys. If something is 14K gold it is 14 parts pure gold and 10 parts alloy, the total is always 24.

British 9 karat gold (Not legal in the USA): 9CT, .225

10 Karat Gold: 10K, 10KP, .375

14 Karat Gold: 14K, 14KP, .585

18 Karat Gold: 18K, 18KP, .750

22 Karat Gold: Not sold in the USA, 22K, 22KP Usually sold in Asia as a means of wearing the gold and being able to take it with you if you need to move to another area.

24 Karat Gold: 24k, .999

Gold Filled is marked to show, by weight, an amount of a gold layer on the outside of base metal. For example, the mark 1/10 14kGF. This means the gold layer is 14k and is 1/10 the weight of the total metal in the item. 1/20 10kGF would likewise mean the gold layer is 10k and it is 1/20 the weight of the total metal in the item.

HGE is Heavy Gold Electroplate (plated, not solid gold) .

GP is Gold Electroplate (plated, not solid gold). Also no mark on many gold plated items.

Vermeil is gold plate, wash or flash over sterling silver. To be properly done a nickel plate is first applied to the sterling and then the gold.

You will note sometimes an item is marked K or KP. If it just K it may be a little less in quality due to rounding off. An item that was 13.5 karat used to be marked 14 karat. The P was later introduced to mean that the item was a full 14K and not rounded. The P stands for Plum. So 14KP means it is full 14K. 10,14,18, etc is the parts of gold in an item 14K would mean 14 parts gold and 10 parts alloy. The total always adds up to 24. 24K is pure gold also called .999 Fine.

Some items are hallmarked OROID -
Oroid is an alloy of copper, zinc, and tin, used in imitation gold jewelry.
Copper - approx. 81 %, tin - approx. 15 %, zinc - approx. 5 %

Other Silver Hallmarks by County / Region

Sterling may not be sterling in another country, no international law was established to determine a set of rules, but rather each country or region may have developed a set of criteria. For example, if you find an insignia stamped 875, it may mean it was made in Estonia or Latvia. Below is a basic list by areas of silver quality hallmarks used in each area.

Australia - Sterlng Silver, STG SIL, or any combination.
Austria - Until 1867 they used a system whit a name of "loth"
12 loth corresponding to 750/1000, 13 loth = 812/1000, 14 loth = 875/1000, 15 loth = 937/1000
After 1867 they used a system called Diana head and a number. This was the head of a woman and a small number. The number corresponded to the following fineness.
1=950/1000 - 2=900/1000 - 3=800/1000 -4=750/1000

Belgium - prior to 1868 .800, 1968 to 1942 A1- was for .900 and A2 for .800 silver

Canada - Sterling, 925

China - would fill a book on its own and has. They used a system of makers marks.

Czech Republic -
Czechoslovakia - A symbol with a letter or number. 1922-1929 A head with a number 4 = .750, 3 = .800, 2 = .900, 1 = .950. 1929 to 1942 a cross with a number 5 = .800, 4 = .835, 3 = .900, 2 = .925 and 1 = .999. After 1942 a pyramid with a number in the center which wss the same as 1929 standard.

Denmark - a number of fineness with a assay and maker marks.

English, Scottish and Irish Silver (most commonwealth countries)
The hallmarks are extremely detailed with different marks for years and locations. A lion passant guardant or Britannia or lion's head erased, certifying the silver quality and 925.

Estonia / Latvia 1920 - 78, 84 -after 1924 - 800, 875, 900, 935 with a makers mark.

France
June 1798 to September 1809
Rooster with number 1- 950
Rooster with number 2 - 800
Head with 85 - 850
Head with 50 - 500
November 1809 to August 1819
Rooster with number 1- 950
Rooster with number 2 - 800
Head with 34 - 340

August 1819 to May 1838
Head facing right with number 1 - 950
Head facing left with number 2 - 800
Head with 34 - 340
Head facing forward - 340
After May 1938
Roman Solder head with a number 1 or 2 - 950
Wild Boar Head or Lobster - 800
French Coin Silver 835

Finland - 916H is actually .935

Germany - Silver fineness was indicated in "loth" (12 loth corresponding to 750/1000, 13 loth = 812/1000, 14 loth = 875/1000, 15 loth = 937/1000). In 1888 the system was changed to a crescent and crown with a number 800, 925.

Hungary - 1937 to 1965, Womens head with a number, 1 = .935, 2 = .900, 3 = .800.

India - basically same as English, but some items will just be marked SILVER

Iran - 84 with maker mark = .875, after 1967 to 1979 a lion with sward is .875 with doube line aroudn the mark = .900.

Italy - 800, 900, 925, 950

Japan - After 1928 started to use a number system for silver ie .925 Sterling and .950 Silver.

Korea - post 1945, Silver with a number in three digits or two digits with or without a percent sign. Such as 99% would be 99 percent pure,

Mexico - Until 1948 Mexican silver was marked silver or sterling. Between 1948 and into the 1980's an Eagle with an ID number was used but many companies bypassed the system. Then they went to an letter ID system and it is still in use. Sterling and 925. You will also items just marked SILVER.

Russia (old) - 84, 88, 91 followed by other marks to show the maker. If only a number is shown the odds are the item is a fake.

WARNING - in the far east in some cases "Sterling" is used for silver plate and "pure Silver" is regarded as .900 silver.

US Military Hallmarks

Prior to 1905-6 hallmarks did not appear on many of the items made for not only the military but also the civilian markets. It was the National Gold and Silver Stamping Act of 1905 that established the concept of hallmarking in the United States. It required that articles made of gold or silver indicate the fineness or quality of the metal. It also set standards of the word "sterling" and forbid its use for plated or layered metals. The item had to solid sterling or solid 14k gold. It went into effect June 13, 1906. The law has basically remain the same over the years with additions for example platinum. What is very interesting is that under this law you did not have to mark an item as to its fineness but you do not need to stamp it on the item itself. You can identify it on the invoice, on a hang tag, or on other descriptive material accompanying the piece. If you do choose to quality stamp the jewelry item made of gold or silver, the law requires that you place a federally registered trademark in close proximity to the quality stamp. This has the effect of providing assurance to the purchaser that the item's precious metal quality is guaranteed by the entity that stamps the item. The manufacturer's duly registered trademark is usually stamped on the product - or the retailer can apply a registered stamp. However few if any companies actually registered their mark with the US Patent Office. In fact during WWII the War Department told insignia manufacturers not to place their hallmark on items purchase for use by the military, just the metal finest.

Military Hallmark Coding

Only three main sets of hallmarks were every used on military insignia and a very brief overview is provided here. Following the overview are the details of each and subsequently are examples and information on each manufacturer.

Pre-Korean War - No real system existed. In WWI and just before WWII each manufacturer would mark their products according to Federal Law. During WWII as already stated the firms under government contract to the various official quartermasters did not have a manufacturers mark but only a metal purity mark as required by the National Gold and Silver Stamp Act. However private, base and fleet exchanges they did meet the requirements of the Act and showed the manufacturers and metal marks.

Korean War (1950)-
    1. USMC Quartermaster started to issue serial numbers for various manufacturers, this is a three digit number except in the case of N.S. Meyer that had a two digit number. One of the confusing issues with this is that the same company can have a number of numbers issued to them. No records have been found that provides a complete listing of all the assigned numbers.

    2. Also during the Korean War era the US Army Institute of Heraldry had manufacturers use a two letter code "GI". This was the IOH's certification mark, not an abbreviation for General Insignia. Speculation has abounded on weather GI stood for General Issue or Government Issue.

1953 - Institute of Heraldry started a one digit/ one letter codes in late 1953 and most came into being in 1954 and lasted until 1964-1965. To confuse matters a few two digit / one letter were also assigned during this time period. But they had the digits in front of the letter for example 12C.

1964-65 After 1965 Institute of Heraldry changed the systems where the letter came first followed by the two digits such as V21.

1967 - For insignia directly assigned to the US Navy an "N" was added to the hallmark for example V21-N would indicate Naval insignia made by Vanguard. But this is not always the case. Sometimes the code may be shown with dashes such as V-21-N. The N designation is assigned by Navy Exchange Tailor Shops, Navy Clothing and Textile Research Facility located at the US Army Natick Laboratory, MA for the Navy. Numbers N40N to N61N are designed direct Naval Numbers. Repeated attempts have been made to get the listings for the manufacturers listed under the US Navy assigned numbers.

U.S. Army
The Institute of Heraldry
9325 Gunston Rd, Room S-113
Ft. Belvoir, Virginia 22060-5579
The mission of IOH is to furnish heraldic services to the Executive Office of the President, the Department of Defense, and all other Federal agencies.
Website: http://www.tioh.hqda.pentagon.mil/default.aspx

U.S. Navy
Navy Clothing and Textile Research Facility
15 Kansas St.
NCTRF/Building 86
Natick, MA 01760-5015
Website: https://www.navsup.navy.mil/navsup/ourteam/nexcom/prod_serv/nctrf

US Marine Corp Quartermaster Insignia Serial Numbers (Certification)

Here are a few of the numbers that are known sometimes the words "Serial Number" would appear on the item. This added to confusion as some assumed it was the serial number of the person having the insignia.

Balfour 821
GEMSCO 220, 298
Hickok 170
H&H Hilborn and Hamburg 135,307,388, 397,362,592,622, 678
N.S. Meyer 97, 210, 270, 593, 719
Officers Equipment Co. 603, 678, 803
Sugerman 501
Vanguard - 154
Wolf 716

Institute of Heraldry List of Concerns Authorized to Manufacturer Military Insignia.

This is a list of all companies, concerns that were authorized as a manufacturer of any type. The following pages dive into each one of these were possible to provide additional information on location and a short history and most importantly hallmarks if they had any.

WARNING this list is not known to be 100% accurate. Most of the concerns on this list are in the book even if no hallmarks could be found. This is the most complete list of its kind. This may be copied but must indicate it is "Copyright Joe Weingarten"

I= Insignia (service arm, branch, distinctive unit, etc.)
M= Medals
W= "Wing" qualification badges (aviation, airborne)

A
A.B. Emblems and Caps (later A. B. Emblems/Conrad Industries), Weaverville, NC. (A35) (textile)
Ace, Japan. I
Ace Schiffli Embroidery Co,
Achievement Products, Inc., East Hanover, NJ. (A30) I
Action Embroidery Corp., Ontario, CA. (A25) (textile)
Active Generation, Dallas TX (A33)
Adriel Brothers, Inc. Attleboro, MA. (A32)
Advantage Emblem Inc., Duluth, MN., (M34)
Aerial Impressions, (A35)
Alberti and Company, Firenze, Italy. I
Alice's Alterations, Jonesboro, GA., (A40)
Allen Uniform Company. I
All State Medal Co.Inc., Lodi, NJ (A38)
Amcraft/American Metal Crafts Co. ("snowflake" pattern) (A26)I, W
American Emblem Company, Utica, NY (AE/AECo). I, M, W
American Embroidery Corp., (A31)
American Identification Products, Brooklyn, NY. (A29) I
American Insignia Company, NY. (Amico, 8A, A22) I, W
American Military Supply Corp., New York. (12A, A28) I
AMS, Chicago, IL
Amico (see American Insignia Company)
Anataya Brothers, Inc., Japan and Attleboro, MA. (A26) I
Angus & Coote, Sydney, Australia. I, W
Anson Inc., Providence, RI (A34)
Anthem Insignia, Inc., Providence, RI (41)
Apollo Jewelry Mfg. Co., aka APOLLO MILITARY MANUF CO. New York. (A27)
F.A. Aquino, Manila, Philippines. I
Charles Arista, Hawaii. (CRA) I
Army-Navy Equipment Co. I
Aronoff Service Products Co., New York. (4A, A23)
F.W. Assman, Ludenscheid, Germany ("A" with extended crossbar). I, W
Augis, Lyon, France. I
D.L. Auld Company, Columbus, OH. I, M

Award Crafters, Inc., Chantilly, VA. (A37) (plaque)
Awards by Wilson Trophy, St. Louis, MO. (A39)
B
Bailey, Banks & Biddle, Philadelphia, PA (BB&B). I, M, W
Baldwin Ribbon & Stamping, Woodside, NY. (B31) (Metal)
L.G. Balfour, Attleboro, MA (LGB, 1B, B21). I, W
The Ball and Socket Co., Cheshire, CT (B27)
Bally Ribbon Mills, Bally, PA. (B22) (textile)
C.Balmberger, Germany. I
J. Balme, Paris. W
Baron, Los Angles, CA., (B29)
BD Corp (B32)
B&A, Mesa, AZ., (B33)
B&U Co., I
Bastian Brothers, Rochester, NY. (B.B.Co.). I, M
Bates & Klinke, Inc., Attleboro, MA. I
Jennot Beanne, France. I
Bee-Kay Parade Equipment Co., Bronx, NY. (14B, B23)
Bell Trading Post (signpost with bell emblem, 7B. Insignia.) W
Bell Products, (B25)
Bende & Sons, Inc., Passaic, NJ. (B26) (textile)
Berben Insignia Co., Philadelphia, PA. (12B)
Arthus Bertrand, Paris, France. I
Joe C. Bettencourt Company, San Antonio, TX. I
Beverly Craft, Beverly Hills, CA. (palm tree logo) W
Biederman Co., Bonn, Germany. I
Wallace Bishop Co., Brisbane, Australia. I, W
B.J. Co. (by Orber). I
V.H. Blackinton Company, Attleboro Falls, MA (VHB, B24). I, W
Blumberg Bros, New York, NY. W
M.S. Bowman, New York City. I
Branded Emblem Co. Overland Park, KS., (B28)
Bregonzio, Milano, Italy. I
Brehmer, Germany. I
Brooks Awards & Medals, Island Park, NY (B35)
Broy Co Manufacturing & Sales Co., West Bend, WI. (B34)
BS&T Corp., North Attlrboro, MA (B30)
Buerge, Germany(?). I
Fritz Buttner & Sohn, Germany. I
C
C&C Metal Products, Englewood, NJ., (C34)
C & P Embroidery Co., Inc., North Bergen, NJ (C27) (textile, shoulder sleeve)
Carolina Emblems Co., Campobello, SC (C28)
Carolina Service Co., Fayetteville, NC. (C25) I
S.D. Childs, Chicago, IL. I
Cindarn Plastics Inc., Balimore, MD., (C28)
Citco. I
CKS, Seoul, South Korea. I
Classic Medallics, Inc., Long Island City, NY. (C31) I
Clayton, Chicago, IL. I
Clover Embroidery Works, (C21)
College Shops, Attleboro, MA. I
Colonial Promotions, (C29)

Colorado Stitchery, Colorado Springs, CO., (C33)
Columbia Button & Nailhead Corp., New York, NY. (C24) I
Cooper Industries, Upland, CA., (C30)
Coro (Cohn & Rosenberger), New York, NY/Providence, RI. (12C, C22)) I, M, W
Cover Stitches, West New York, NY (C35)
Craftens Inc., Chicago, IL. I
Creative Modeling & Die Mfg. Co., North Attleboro, RI., (C32)
Crest-Craft Co., Cincinnati, OH. (C23) I

D

Danecraft, Inc., Providence, RI. W
Freeman Daughaday Co.(Norton, MA through 1946, then Providence, RI) M
The Dawson Company, Cleveland, OH. I
Delancy School of Marketing (D24)
Denazio, Corizia, Italy. I
Denmark's Military Equipment Corp., New York/Astoria, NY. (6D, D22) I
A.J. Dennison, Riverside, RI. (5D, D23) I
Deschler & Sohn, Munich, Germany. I
Designer Tool & Die, Seekok, MA.,(D27)
Detail Manufacturing Co, Inc., (D26)
Diana"s Flag & Guidons, Killeen, TX., (D28)
Dieges & Clust, New York. I, M
Discovery Marketing & Design Ltd., Pawtucket, RI (D29)
Diversified Metal Crafters Inc., Lincoln, RI (30)
Diversified Products Inc. Providence PI (D25)
Dobbins. I
Dodge Inc., Chicago, IL. I
Dodge Trophy Co., Los Angeles, CA. I
Dohmer, Germany. (D1) I
Dommers, Germany. I
A.H. Dondero, Washington. (D2, D21) I, W
Donner, Elberfeld, Germany. I
N.C. Dorrety, Boston, MA. I
Durocharm, New York City. I
Dan H. Dunham, San Antonio, TX. W
C.B. Dyer. I

E

Eagle Crest, Jacksonville, FL (E33)
Eagle Regalia Co., New York. (E24) I
Eagle Tool Inc., Providence, RI (E35)
S.E. Eby, Philadelphia, PA. I, M, W
Ebsco Industries, Inc., Birmingham, AL. (E28) I
Eisenstadt Jewelry Co, St. Louis, MO (LE). I, W
Eiseman-Ludmar Co., Inc., Hicksville, NY. (E31) (bullion)
Elco Embroidery Works (E22)
Elden Industries, Cranston, RI., (E32)
Elwyn Industries Inc., Elwyn, PA., (E29)
Emblem and Badge Co., Providence, RI. (E21) I
Emblemcraft Ltd, New York, NY. (E25) I
Emblem Supply Co., Inc., Central Falls, RI. (1E, E23) I
Empire State Metal Products, Richmond Hill, NY., (E34)
Erffmeyer & Son, Ind., Milwaukee, WI. (E27) I (2*)
Eveready Embroidery, Inc., Jersey City, NJ. (E26) (1#)
Everson Ross Co., Spring Valley, NY., (E30)

F
Fawn Industries Inc., New Park, PA. (F24)
FBF Industries Inc., Southampton, PA., (F26)
Finishing Touch Embroideries, West New York, NY. (F26)
Firmin & Sons, London, England. W
Bruce Fox Inc., New Albany, NY. nn
Gustave Fox Co., Cincinnati, OH. I, W
M. Fox Inc., Woodstock, VT. (F23)
Frielich Brothers (F21N)
August Frank. M
Frank Brothers, San Antonio, TX. (2F) I
Lorioli Fratelli, Milano, Italy. I
Thomas Frattorinin, Birmingham, England. I
John Frick Jewelry Co., New York. I
Fulford Manufacturing Co., (F22)
G
Master Craft Awards and General Display Co., Manassas, VA. (G25)
Samual Gallini, New York, NY., (G29N)
Gamber Products Co. Inc., Warwick, RI., (G30)
J.R. Gaunt & Son, London, England/New York, NY. I, W
Gemsco (General Embroidery and Military Supply Company), Milford, CT. (G2, G22) I,W
General Display Co., Manassas, VA. (G25) (plaque)
General Insignia, New York, NY. I
General Products, Providence, RI. M
George & Sidney's Brass Shop, Taipei, Taiwan (G&S Co). I
Gerocastelli (Gero Castelli?), Italy. I
Ges. Gesh. (Not a company; German patent mark). I
George S. Gethen Co., Philadelphia, PA. I
GGFXA (S.E. Eby Co.?). I
GJM Manufacturing, Attleboro, RI., (G32)
Gleason-Wallace, Albany, NY. I
Goodwear Fabrics
Gordon's Fort Meade, Odenton, MD. (G13) I
Graco Awards, Tomball, TX. (G27) M (2)
M.M. Graham, Los Angeles. I
Grannat Brothers, San Francisco, CA. I
Great American Weaving Corp., Bally, PA (G31) (1)
Greenduck, Chicago, IL. I
The Green Company, Kansas City, MO. I (Green KC, 6G, G26). I (5*#)
Ira Greene Co., New York, NY/Providence, RI. (3G, G3, G23) I
The Gross Organization, Fort Worth, TX., (G28)
H
V. Haacke & Co., Pforzheim, Germany. I
Irvin H. Hahn Company, Baltimore (Hanco/rooster logo, 1H, H22). I
Hallmark Emblems, Inc. (H27) (1#)
Haltom Jewelers, Fort Worth, TX. W
Alvin H. Hankins, Seattle, WA. I
Harding (Newell Harding & Co.?), Boston, MA. I
Hartegen, Newark, NH. I
Hardmann Inc., (H23)
A.J. Hawkins. I
H.E. Heacock Co., Manila, Philippines. I
B. Hecker, New York. I

Heckethorn Mfg. & Supply Co., Littleton, CO. M
Jack Heller ("H" in a circle?) (H21)
Wilhelm Helding, Leipzig, Germany. I
Henderson-Ames Co., Kalamazoo, MI. I
Herndon Recognition, Portland, OR., (H34)
Hess & Albertson, St. Louis, MO. I
Michael Hessberg, (H32N)
Hilborn-Hamburger, New York, NY/Passaic, NJ. (H-H/eagle logo, H-H Imperial, H24). I, M
High Flight, Rancho, CA., (H26)
Cal Hirsch & Sons Iron and Rail Co., St. Louis, MO. I
G. Hirsch & Sons (H31N)
His Lordship's Products, Inc., New York, NY. (H25, LI. L22))
Hook-Fast Specialties Inc., Providence, RI., (H33)
Horstmann, Philadelphia, PA. I
Humrichous Co, Memphis, TN. (HR). W

I
Imperial Insignia Manufacturing Company (later Hilborn-Hamberger/Imperial). I
Inter-all Corp Granby, MA. (I24)
Internationl Enterprises Ltd, Providence, RI., T21
International Insignia Corp., Providence, RI. (I21) I (2*)
Interstate Lace Co., Union City, NJ. (I23)
Irvine & Jachens, San Francisco, CA. I
Ivy Emblems Corp. North Bergen, NJ. (I22)

J
Jacqueline Embroidery Co., Toms River, NJ. (J23) (textile)
Jaurez. W
Warren Jay Products Corp., New York, NY. (1J) I
JayMac Bowling Supplies, Eire, PA., (J22)
Jostens, Inc., Princeton, IL/Owatonna & Minneapolis, MN. I, W
Johnson National, New York. I
Joy Insignia, Inc., Deerfield Beach, FL., (J21)

K
Acute Ides(S)/ Ira K. Medals, Marietta, GA., (K28)
Kaag, Los Angeles. I
Martin Kahn, Bronx, NY. (6K)
Kalka, Augsburg, Germany. I
K. B. Specialties, Bellflower, CA (KBS, K25). I
Kel-Lac Uniforms Inc., San Antonio, TX., (K27)
Kennedy Inc., North Kingstown, RI., (K28)
William C. Kiff Co., (K22)
The Kinney Co. Providence, RI ("K Co." in a shield, K24) W
Harry Klitzner Co., Inc., Providence, RI., (K26)
Klammer, Innsbruck, Austria. I
Karl J. Klein, Portland, OR. I
Konwal (Western Military Supply), Japan. I
Krew,Inc.,Attleboro,MA. (1K, K21) I, M, W
G. Kugelmann Co./ Guaynabo Corp., College Point, NY., (K23)

L
The Walter Lampl Co. (script "WL" in a shield), New York, NY. W
Laorer, Los Angeles, CA. I
L. Christian Lauer, Nurnberg, Germany. I
Leary's Military Co., Wilmington, DE., (L28)
Leavens Manufacturing Co., Attleboro, MA. (L21) I

Leonard Embroidery Company, Philadelphia, PA. (2L, L23) I
Letters Medals Inc., San Juan, PR., (L29)
LeVelle, Philadelphia, PA/Washington, D.C. I, W
Liberty Insignia Corp., Amherst, NY., (L27)
William Link & Co. ("WL Co" in 2 linked ovals) W
Linz Brothers Jewelers, Dallas, TX. W
Lion Brothers Co. Inc., Owings Mill, MD., (L26)
Loma-Linda Cherrco, Redlands, CA., (L24)
HLI Lordship Industries, Inc., Hauppauge, NY. (H25, L1, L22) M
Los Angeles Rubber Stamp Co., Los Angeles, CA (LARS). I
Louisville Mfg Co., (L25)
Ludlow Co., London, England. W
K. G. Luke Co., Melbourne, Australia. W
W. Lutz, Furth, Germany. I
Morrie Luxenberg, New York, NY. I, W

M

Maacs Inc., Wells, ME., (M38)
Maco-Boch
Magic Novelty Co., Inc., New York, NY., (M30)
S. Mars,
Jerry Massey. W
Joseph Mayer. M
Jos. Mayr, Linz, Austria. I
McAllister Industries, Inc. (M35)
McCabe Brothers, New York, NY. (M23) I
Gordon's Fort Meade, Odenton, MD. (M24) I
Medals of America, Fountain Inn, SC., (M37)
Medallic Art Co., New York, NY. I, M
The Metal Craft Mint, Inc., Green Bay, WI., (M33)
Merit Ribbon Co., (M26)
Mermod, Jaccard & King, St. Louis, MO. I
Metal Arts Co., Rochester, NY. (AMACO, M30). I
G.C.Meyer Company, Indianapolis, IN. I
N.S. Meyer, New York, NY. (9M, M22) I, M, W
Meyers & Co., Los Angeles. I
Midwest Trophy Co., Del City, OK. (M29) I
Mil-Bar Plastics Inc., Corona, CA., (M39)
Military Art & Emblem Co., Hyattsville, MD. (M29) I
Military Equipment Corp. Mossistown, NJ., (M32N)
Military Manufacturer's of Maryland (by Gordon's Fort Meade). (G18, M24))
Military Post Suppliers, Japan/Newark, NJ. (7M, M7, M21) I
J. Milton, New York. I
Minero-Newcome, Co, New York, NY. (1M, M28) I
Minister, Columbus, OH. I
Monarch Military Products Co., Inc. New York, NY. (M12) I
Moody Bros., Los Angeles, CA. W
Morgan's, San Francisco, CA. I
Motex Inc., West New York, NJ. (M36) (textile)
Mourgeon, France. I
Loren Murchison & Co., Attleboro, MA. (M27) I

N

National Badge & Insignia Co., Japan/Washington, DC. (NBI Japan) I
National Decoration Co., Shanghai, China (NDC). I

National Die & Button Mold, Carlstadt, NJ., (N28)
National Emblem & Embroidery (N21)
National Emblem & Badge, Carson, CA., (N27)
National Guard Equipment Company, New York. (NGBC). I
Naval Uniform Supply (NUS). W
N.B.I., Japan. I
Nellie's Alterration & Manufacturing, Mountain Brook, AL., (N29)
Nelson, Long Beach, NY. I
N. R. Newcome & Co., New York, NY. I
New England Trophy & Engraving Co., Boston, MA. (N22) I
Newtel Inc., Miami, FL., (N24N)
Niderost & Taber. I
C.W. Nielson Mfg Corp., Chehals, WA., (N25)
F. H. Noble & Co. Chicago, IL. (Letter "N" in a circle) M
Ken Nolan Inc., Irvine, CA., (N23N)
Norsid Co., New York, NY. W
The North Attleboro Jewelry, Co., Attleboro, MA., (N30)
Northern Stamping Co. M
Northeast Emblem & Badge, Cheshire, CT.
Northwest Territory Mint, Auburn, WA (N31) (2, 7)
Nudelman Bros. I
N- Note Numbers N40N thru N61N were assigned to the US Navy Clothing and Textile Research Facility

O

The Oak Basket, Laurel, MS., (O24)
J. O'Brien Badge Co. (JO?). W
Officers Equipment Co., Madison, NJ. (OEC, OEC14-81) I
Officers Equipment Co., Stafford, VA ., (O22)
Olympic Trophy & Awards Co., Chicago, IL. (O23)
Oppenstein Brothers, Kansas City, MO. I
Orber Manufacturing Co., Garden City, RI. (1O, O1, O21) I, W
RS Owens & Co., Chicago, IL., (O25)

P

E.P. Industries, Inc., Cranston, RI. (P23) I
C. Pacagnini, Milano, Italy. I
Paramount Jewelers, San Francisco, CA . I
Paramount Manufacturing Co., Sanborn, NY., (P31)
Parry & Parry, Salt Lake City, UT. I
Pasquale Uniform Company, San Francisco, CA. (3P) I, W
Patriot Identity, Attleboro, MA., (P32)
Patriot Insignia, Bohemia, NY., (P29)
Pauls, Buffalo, NY. I
Pecas Embroidery Corp., North Bergen, NJ. (P25) (textile)
Peerless Embroidery Co., Chicago, IL (P28)
Penn Emblem, Co., Philadelphia, PA., (P27)
Ed Pereia Inc., Foster, RI. (P24) I
Personally Yours, Wenatchee, WA., (P26)
Philadelphia Badge Co., Philadelphia, PA. I
Pichiani-Barlacci, Firenze, Italy. I
Pichelklammer, Innsbruck, Austria. I
Pieces of History, Cave Creek, AZ (P30)
E.P. Industries, Inc., Providence, RI. I
Carl Poellath, Schrobenhausen, Germany. (P in a circle). I

Polar Flight. W
C. Polk Co./Polk Sales Corp., New York, NY. (CP&Co, 1P, P21) I, W
Pollack Co. I
Prefax Inc., (P22)
Preisser, Pforzheim, Germany. I
Princeton Industries, Inc., Providence, RI. I
R
Rainbow Emblems, Ind., Johnson, RI. (R25) I
Rainbow Embroidery, East Brunswick, NJ. (R27) (textile)
Ray Inc., Houston, TX., (R26)
Regal Emblem Co. Inc., New York. (R23) I
Regimental Sig Co., Washington, DC., (R31)
Reliable World Trade Co. Inc., Oakland, CA., (R30)
Alois Rettenmaier, Germany. I
Rex Products. M
The Reynolds Co., Lincoln, RI. (R24) I
Ricci, Firenze, Italy. I
C. Ridabock & Co., New York. I
River City Pattern Inc., Clackamas, OR (R29)
Rixtine, Lincoln, NB. I
R.K. & Co., Calcutta, India. I
Charles R. Robbins Company, Attleboro, MA (R in diamond w/wings, R21). I, W
Rocky Mountain Memorabilia (R28)
Roland I
Rosenfield, Boston, MA. I
Rota, Genoa, Italy (R). I
The Roulet Company, Toledo, OH. I
The Rowland Company, Philadelphia, PA. I
D. J. Ryan Inc., (R22)
Russell Uniform Co., New York. I
S
V. Saracino, Taranto, Italy. I
Sayre Enterprises, Buena Vista, VA (S44) (1)
Schiffli Corp of America, (S27)
Schreyer Embroidery Co., Fairview, NJ. (S33) (textile) (1#)
Schriade J.M. Schriade, Chicago, IL. I
Schwertner & Cie, Graz Eggenberger. I
Schweizer Emblem Co., Park Ridge, IL., (S41)
Shalhoub Brothers (S28)
Sherman Manufacturing Co., Providence, RI. (3S, S24) I
Shreve & Co., San Francisco, CA. W
Ben Silver, Inc., Manhasset, NY. (S30) I
Silverman Bros./ Silverman Corp. (S22) M
Simba Awards, Ltd., Long Island, NY. (S35) I
Simco/E.H. Simon Co. (diamond with vertical lightning). I, M
Simon and Sons, Ltd. (SS Ltd), England. W, I
Wm. J. Siravo Designs Inc., Buena Vista, VA., (S43)
N.G. Slater Corp., New York, NY, (S31) I
Daniel Smilo & Sons, New York, NY. M
Smart Design Inc., Woodbridge, VA., (51)
Smith & Warren, White Plains, NY (50)
Snag-Prufe Fasteners, Louisville, KY. (S25) I

Spies Brothers, Chicago, IL. I
Sports Caddy LLC, Charlotte, NC (S45)
Stabilimenti Artistici, Firenze, Italy. I
Stadri Emblem Inc., Woodstock, NY (S42)
Standard Manufacturing Co. (S23)
Starcrest (primarily "made for collector" and veteran's pieces)
Stay Bright Products, Baltimore, MD (S39)
Stay Sharp Tool C. Inc., North Attleboro, MA, (S34)
Stefano Johnson, Milan, Italy. I
Stempel-Schutz, Darmstadt, Germany . I
Stitch Gallery Inc. Harlington, TX., (S48)
Stitchin Post, Bradenton, FL., (S49)
Strange Co., (S36)
Franz Sturies, Germany. I
Harry Sugerman/Susco. (S21) I
Sun Badge Co. Sna Dimas, CA., (S47)
Superior Die & Stamping Inc., Norton MA., (S46)
Supreme Military Insignia (S26)
The Supply Room, Anniston, AL. (S38) I
Sussman. I
Sutton Manufacturing (S37)
Swank, Inc., Attleboro, MA. M
Swiss Maid Inc., Greentown, PA (S40)
Swiss-Tex Corp. (S29)
T
O.C. Tanner, Salt Lake City, UT. W
A&S Taub, Belleview, IL
T&P. I
Taxco. W
TC Art & Crafts Works, Honolulu, HI., (T22)
Telepunch Inc, Palatine, IL (T25)
Thomas Co., Attleboro, MA. I
Tiffany & Co., New York. I, W
Tommy Tucker T-Shirts, Tucson, AZ., (T24)
Tucker Shean, Lincoln, NB. I
U
Uncas Mfg. Co., Providence, RI. (Letter "U" with arrow through it.) M
United Emblem Co., New York, NY. I
United Military, New York, NY. (6U) I
United UniformAccesspries Inc., Long Island City, NY., (U22)
Universal Specialty Awards Inc., Pawtucket, RI (U23)
Uris Sales Corporation, New York. (4U) I
Urschel Tool Corp. Cranston, RI. (U21) I
U.S. Infantry Association, Washington, DC. I
U.S. Specialty Co., New York, NY. I
V
A. Valcan, Japan (AA in quotes). I
W. A. Valdez, Philippines. I
Vanalen Company, New York and Kansas City, MO. I
Vanguard Military Equip. Co/Vanguard Insignia Co., Brooklyn/NYC/Norfolk, VA/Carlsbad, CA. (1V, V21)I, W
Van Wormer & Rodrigues, San Francisco, CA. I
Vargas Manufacturing Company, Providence, RI. Horizontal diamond with superimposed "V".

First use 1947. I
VHB (see V. H. Blackinton)
Volupte, Inc., New York, NY. I, M
Voyager Emblems, Sanborn, NY., (V22)
Vulcan, Tokyo, Japan ("AT" in heart). I
Vulcan Industries, Birmingham, AL. I
W
The Wallace Co., Inc., Providence, RI. (2W)
C.H. Wallbank Company, Brookline, MA. I
Wallenstein. I
Warner Woven Label Co., Paterson, NJ (W24)
Warwick Emblem Supply, Warwick, RI. (W30) I (2*)
Waterbury Companies, Inc., Waterbury, CT M (W21)
Wehing Bro's Mfg., Detroit, MI. W
Weidmann, Frankfurt, Germany. I
Weingarten Gallery, Dayton, OH/Indianapolis, IN. (W32) I, W.
Wellington, Tokyo, Japan. I
Wendell & Co., Chicago, IL. I
Wendll's Inc., Chicago, IL (W31)
Western Military Supply Co., Japan/San Francisco, CA. (W23) I
Weyhing. W
Whitehead and Hoag, Newark, NJ. ("WH" in a shield) I, M, W
Whittemore and Company, Attleboro, MA. I
Wichman, Honolulu, HI. I
Wick Embroidery Co., Union City, NY (W26)
F.M. Wickham. I
Wil-Tex Industries, Patterson, NJ, (W28)
Williams & Anderson Co., Providence, RI. (WACO). (W25) I
Williams & Sons, (W27)
Windsor Gramercy Corp., New York, NY. (W29)
Wolf Appleton Co., New York, NY (WA-NY). W
Wolf-Brown, Inc., Los Angeles, CA. (W22) I
J. R. Wood Products Corp. M
Wright and Street, Chicago, IL. I
Y
Yorktowne Sports Inc., Cockeysville, MD., (Y21)
Z
Crispulo Zamora, Manila, Philippines. I
Zart's Inc., Pawtucket, RI. (Z21) I

AB Emblems / Conrad Inds.

IOH A35

291 Merrimon Avenue
Weaverville, NC 28787
Phone: 888-438-6773
Fax: 828-658-3581
Web: http://www.abemblem.com

A-B Emblems is a manufacturer of emblems and patches for military, government, corporate and organizations. The company began as a manufacturer of military emblems in World War II founded in 1944.

Ace Novelty
PO Box 1374
Tokyo, Japan

Ace was a patch maker in the 1960's and supplied patches to USAF into the Vietnam period. They had a sticker on the back of their patches as shown. They were in black, copies were later made with the sticker in yellow.

The Ace Schiffli Embroidery Co.
Opa Locka, FL (formerly from New Jersey)

A large government contract embroiderer closed its doors in October 1998 and has gone out of business. The company was charged with conspiracy to suppress and eliminate competition in Federal Court September 1996.

Achievement Products, Inc.   IOH - A30
294 State Route 10
East Hanover, NJ. 07936
(973) 887-5090
http://achievementproducts.com/
Custom trophy's, name plates, patches are listed on their web site.

Active Generation   IOH - A33
AKA   Dallas Cap & Emblem Mfg., Inc.
2924 Main St
Dallas TX 75226
CAGE 6F111
Appeared to be in business from mid 1970's to late 1980's.

Action Embroidery Corp   IOH - A25
1315 W. Brooks St.
Ontario, CA 91762
(800) 638-7223
http://www.actionembroiderycorp.com
Founded in 1943 as Art Embroidery by Mr. Harry Silna in New Jersey. Action moved its facilities to Ontario, California in 1986 and in 1998 Action expanded its operations to include a facility outside of Miami, Florida.

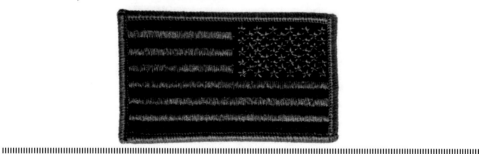

Adriel Brothers, Inc.   IOH A32
107 Frank Mossberg Dr
Attleboro, MA 02703
617-285-3147
Metal stamping company. No current information.

Advantage Emblem Inc. IOH M34
4313 Haines Rd.
Duluth, MN 55811
Established in 1994 as an emblem company now has expended into banners and screen printing. Still in business.

Aerial Impressions IOH A36
No information on this concern.

Alberti & Co.
Firenze, Italy. I
Milan, Italy
Produced insignia during the early years of the occupation period after WWII.

Alice's Alterations IOH A40
500 Quartermaster Rd
Jonesboro, GA 10738
It appears this company is no longer in business and was purchased by AB Emblem.

George Alan Co
6800 Distribution Drive
Beltsville, Maryland 20705
Founded in 1948 and still in business however no longer makes or provides any insignia. They now are focused on office supplies and technology.

Allen Uniform Company
511 Westminster St
Providence, RI

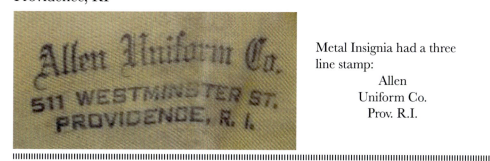

Metal Insignia had a three line stamp:
>Allen
>Uniform Co.
>Prov. R.I.

All State Medal Co. Inc.   IOH A38
16 Adams Place
Lodi, NJ 07644
http://www.allstatemedal.com

A metal stamping and jewelry company founded in the early 1930's. Still in operation.

Amcraft/American Metal Crafts Co.   IOH A26
("snowflake" pattern)

Founded by Thomas Kelliher, an Irish immigrant, American Metalcrafts Company (Amcraft), Inc. of Attleboro, Massachusetts, formerly the American Emblem & Badge Company, was formed in 1918 and was incorporated in 1923 and was in business to the late 1940's when it became a division of the Hilborn-Hamburger Company. American Metalcraft manufactured plated items such as badges, emblems, pins, and belt buckles. It is estimated that the facility was operating between 1948 and 1998 at 53 Falmouth St, Attleboro, MA for H&H.

American Emblem

IOH 1A

Utica, NY
aka - AE or AECo)
The Company was founded in 1914, incorporated Feb 1917 and in September 1917 they build a factory in Utica where the company remain until July 1963 when they were sold to Worcester (Mass.) Stamped Metal Co. The building they were in was to be torn down for a highway and they were unable to find another location in Utica. After WWII they had a struggle to keep going in the insignia business, for example in 1955 the company made nameplates for the Oldsmobile due to the lack of military business.

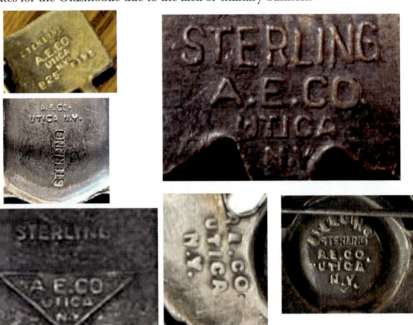

American Embroidery

IOH A31

No information on this company.

American Identification Products

IOH A29

145 58th St,
Brooklyn, NY, 11220-2515
718-492-3400
Cage Code 51790
Founded in 1972 and still in business as an etcher of plaques.

American Insignia Co, NY. (Amico)   IOH   8A, A22

Records show the company was in existence in 1922 and had an IOH identification mark of 8A which means we know it went out of business prior to 1965.

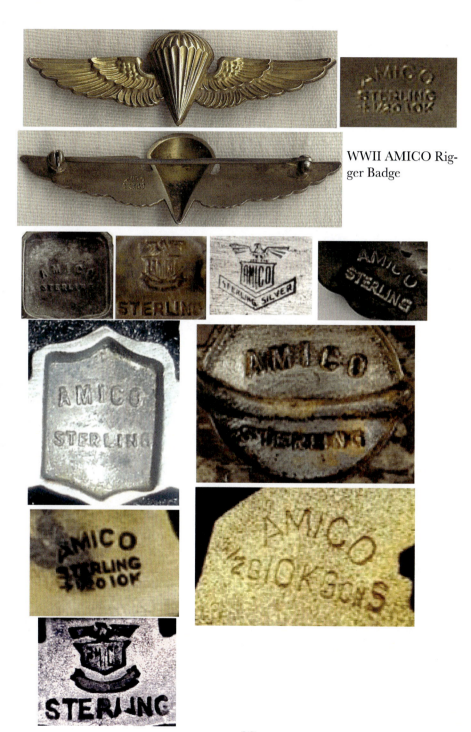

WWII AMICO Rigger Badge

American Military Supply Corp.   IOH 12A, A28
New York.
Founded in 1872 and was a maker / importer of swords. Believed to have gone out of business in the early 1970's. A new company with the same name currently operates out of Macon GA but is just a sales outlet ie "outfitters" and not related to this listing.

AMS
Chicago, IL
No information on this company. This raise logo was on a hat badge which appears to have been made by J R Gaunts and Sons.

Anataya Brothers, Inc.   IOH A26
3 Falmouth St
Attleboro, MA
Founded in 1948 by Donald and John Anataya, Jr. and their father John Antaya, Sr. In 1951 they purchased the equipment of W&R Co. Their primary products were religious items.

Federal Trademark filed
1962 - 0744070

Angus & Coote
Sydney, Australia

Founded in 1895 and still in business and remains one of the most trusted jewelers in Australia. Made insignia for US service personnel stationed in that country during WWII.

Anson Inc.   IOH A34
100 Dupont Dr
Providence, RI 02907
508-222-3600

Founded in 1938 by Swedish immigrant Olaf Anson as a tool and die company, the firm began manufacturing men's jewelry after World War II. This company ceased operation on October 12, 1993.

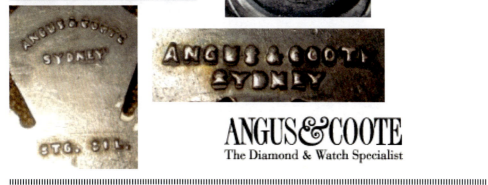

Anthem Insignia Inc. IOH A41
306 Valley St
Providence, RI 02908
610-845-2211
CAGE 4B1T8
The company is listed as a steel metal rolling company and no other information is available. It is still in operation.

Aoki Metals
48-1, Odakacho, Midori-Ku
Nagoya, Aichi 459-8001
Japan
25-1, Narimasu 3-chome, Itabashi-ku,
Tokyo 175-0094, Japan
No longer active in manufacturing military insignia. Currently they are a metal stamping concern.

J. Ando
Tokyo, Japan
No additional information on this concern.

Apollo Jewelry Mfg. Co. IOH A27
264 39th St
Brooklyn, NY 11323
617-222-2611
No additional information on this concern.

A.F. Apple Co
120 East Chestnut St
Lancaster, PA

The company was founded in 1893 by Mr.. J. F. Apple and appears to have ceased operations on September 12, 1952 when they were purchased by New Concern. They were a manufacturer of class and fraternity jewelry and did make some US insignia.

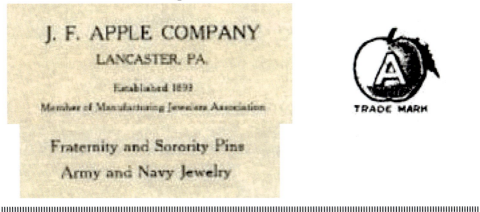

F.A. Aquino
Manila, Philippines.
No additional information on this concern.

Aresta
Charles Aresta
1813 Sereno St.
Honolulu HI, 96817-2318

Charles Arista has been making reproductions of hard to find DIs for veterans reunions and collectors for several years with the Aresta of Hawaii or Charles Aresta, Hawaii. (CRA) mark.

Army-Navy Equipment Co
No information on this company.

Aronoff Service Products Co. IOH 4A, A23
New York.
No information on this company.

Assmann & Sohne, F.W. Assman, Ludenscheid, Germany ("A" with extended crossbar)

Assmann started in the 18th century producing at that time metal buttons for the clothing industry and as well medal decorations for the military. During WWII they were a major supplier of Nazi insignia and after the war starting making US insignia for occupation forces. Each US insignia had a number along with the A to identify its catalog number. Today they are no longer in the insignia business but rather in heat sinks and connectors for electronics.

Some Assman products had a catalog number on each item for example 106 is the code for Lt. Col and 340 for the 2 inch Command Pilot.

Some Assman Catalog codes
106 -Lt Col.
340 - 2 inch Command Pilot
345, 346 2inch Bombardier
320 - 3 inch Command Pilot
266 - Basic Paratrooper   267 - Master Paratrooper
211 Sharpshooter

Associate Military Stores
Chicago, IL and New York, NY
Founded at Camp Lewis WA in 1917. They became a supplier to Base Exchanges and last known advertisement was in the 1930's.

Augis
Lyon, France. I

In 1830 Eugene Coquais founded in Lyon a jewelry store. In 1870 is son Charles succeeded him. In 1896, Alphonse Augis, son of Charles, took over from his father and gave his name to the company that becomes A.Augis. In 1907, one of his successors, Alphonse created A Augis, a factory dedicated to making military badges. Beginning in 1928, the company management was taken over by Franck Augis, son of Alphonse, who turned it over in 1970 to Guy Augis.

A.Augis today is part of the Arthus-Bertrand group and directed by Franck Augis, representing the sixth generation at the head of this family business.

WWII

WWI

Post WWII

D. L. Auld Company
5th Ave & 5th Street
Columbus, OH. I, M

Founded in 1870 by Civil War veteran Demas Auld as a jewelry shop in Columbus, OH. The business became one of the largest companies to made automobile nameplates with the Ford blue oval being their most famous. During World War II, the company retooled to support the war effort and made the Distinguished Service Medal, fragmentation bombs, aluminum forging for military aircraft and dummy planes that were set on military airfields as decoys. Currently still in business as Auld Technologies.

1922 Hallmark

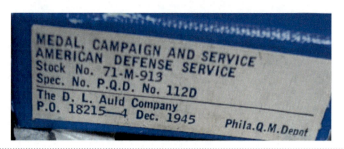

Award Crafters, Inc.　　　　　　　　　　　　　　　　IOH A37
4449-C Brookfield Corporate Dr
Chantilly, VA. 20151
703-818-0500

http://www.awardcrafters.com

Founded in 1964 with a primary focus in making recognition items such as plaques. Still in business.

Awards by Wilson Trophy　　　　　　　　　　　　　IOH A39
9495 Aerospace Dr
St Louis, MO 63134   203-250-6000

Founded in 1955 and appears to still be in business on a smaller scale. Trophies and awards.

Bailey, Banks & Biddle
Philadelphia, PA (BB&B). I, M, W

Founded on September 20, 1832 by Joseph Trowbridge Bailey and Andrew B. Kitchen. In 1840 Mr. Kitchen pasted away and in 1846 Mr. E. W. Bailey joined the concern and it was renamed Bailey and Co. In 1854 Joseph Bailey died and in 1856 his son Joseph Bailey II who had join the business in 1851 became a full partner. It was in 1878 that George Banks and Samuel Biddle formed the partnership of Bailey, Banks and Biddle and 1894 they incorporated to become Bailey, Banks and Biddle Co. In 1962 the company was sold to Zale Corporation and then sold again to Finlay Enterprises in 2007. They filed for Chapter 11 bankruptcy in August 2009. In 2010 it was sold to Mr. Paul Leonard.

The hallmark BBB or BB&B was used more on military items and their full name on commercial products.

Baldwin Ribbon & Stamping   IOH   B31
3956 63rd St,
Woodside, NY 11377
(718) 335-6700 or (888) 335-6900
http://www.baldwinribbon.com/

After World War II, Baldwin Silver was formed by Louis Steinberg with his two partners, and at the time solely focused on silver-smithing and jewelry work. As the years passed, the business expanded and became Baldwin Ribbon & Stamping Corp. in 1985 Louis' son Ronald took over ownership. In 2010, Ronald's son, Eric, joined the company full-time. Currently, they employ over 25 well-trained personnel with many years of experience metal stamping and ribbon production. With skills developed from smithing background, it became an easy transition to medal and award product manufacturing.

L.G. Balfour   IOH 1B, B21
Attleboro, MA. I, W

Founded in 1913 by Lloyd Garfield Balfour, Joseph R Brooks and August V. Friensehner in Attleboro MA. Went out of business in 1996 when it combined with CJC Holdings, Inc to become part of Commemorative Brands, Inc

BALFOUR and LGB hallmarks seem to have been used concurrently.
According to the trademark office, BALFOUR was first used in 1913, but did not apply for trademark protection till 1947 (granted 1949).

WWII - 1959

1954 - 1965

The Ball & Socket Mfg. Co. IOH B27
493 W. Main St
Cheshire, CT 06410
914-679-6600
Ball & Socket (B&S), Cheshire, CT, manufactured metallic buttons and fasteners from the 1850s until September 1994. The factory remained vacant for years and now is a community and arts center.

Edgar F. Baton
722 Chestnut Street
Philadelphia, PA
Established in 1856 by Edgar F Baton it is not known when he stopped operations. Ad shows he was involved in manufacturing military insignia.

BD Corp   IOH B32
No information exist about this listing.

B & A   IOH B33
10510S Lyn Rae Sq
Mesa, AZ
913-648-7920
No information exist about this listing.

B. A. Ballou & Co. Inc.
Founded in 1876 by Barton A Ballou. The company became know for its findings and jewelry. Many of the backs of military insignia have soldered onto them Ballou findings. In 2009 Ballou had been closed after being put into receivership. It later reopened, and its assets were sold to W.R. Cobb.

1922 Hallmark

Bally Ribbon Mills   IOH B22
23 North Seventh St
Bally, PA 19503
610-845-2211
http://www.ballyribbon.com
Since 1923, Bally Ribbon Mills has been involved in the design, development, and manufacture of highly specialized engineered woven webbing, tapes, and specialty fabrics for: aerospace, defense, medical, safety, automotive, commercial, and industrial applications.

C.Balmberger
Germany. I

Manufacturer of NAZI insignia continued in business after the war with contracts from the US Army.

J. Balme

44 Rue De Rouen
Saumur, Maine et Loire 49400
France

J Balme was registered as a business on June 11, 1956. In the early 1980's they made various US insignia in conjunction with Phillips Publishing. Their badges are highly detailed and not many designs were made. They tried to enter the US market but ran into "buy US laws" in trying to sell to the US military. In 2010 they appeared to have gone into bankruptcy and in 2012 started up again as the New Society J Balme as a manufacture of coins and medals.

B&U Co.

It appears this was an Italian company that may have had US Army contracts post WWII to manufacture insignia.

Bastian Brothers (B.B.Co.). I, M

Rochester, NY.   www.bastiancompany.com

Bastian Company was founded in 1895 and was incorporated as Bastian Brothers Company initially operating as a jewelry store. In addition to other products they are also known for police and fire badges. Which would explain the WWII connection to making insignia. They were one of the first union shops and this would explain the union logos on some of their items. They are still in business.

1922

The other hallmarks on these items are marks from the Unions in the BB Shops.

Bates & Klinke, Inc.
Attleboro, MA. I
B&J Manufacturing Corporation
55 Constitution Drive
Taunton, MA 02780
(508) 822-1990

Bates & Klinke, Inc. was founded in 1919 in Attleboro Massachusetts by Harold Bates & Oscar Klinke. Attleboro was a major center for jewelry production in the early 20th century. Bates & Klinke are noted for making souvenir silver charms from tourist travel destinations, along with souvenir spoons, brass souvenir plates, medals, key chains, & military insignia. Most of the travel charms were produced in the 1940s. Today the company does business as B&J Manufacturing Corporation.

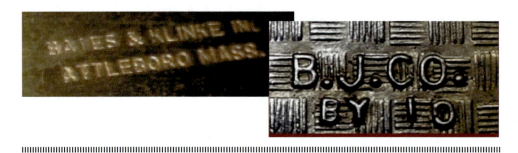

Bauring Jewelers
Long Island City, NY

Founded in the 1930's by a Mr. Baur and Mr. Ring. They were high end jewelers. The hallmark was unusual in that the "ing" was used for both the name and sterling. Beau was used until 1943 then the ing mark was used after the death of Mr. Ring until they appeared to have gone out of business around 1949.

Jennot Beanne   Jeannot - Beaune
France

Post WW ll 324th Fighter Group theater made DI crest pin

Bee-Kay Parade Equipment Co.   IOH 14B, B23
Bronx, NY.
226 Barton Ave
Melville, NY 11747
631-454-9111
www.beekay.com
Founded in 1948 and still in business.

Bell & Brinkner
503 5th Ave
New York NY

Bell Trading Post (signpost with bell emblem)   IOH 7B
The Bell Trading Company was founded in Albuquerque, New Mexico in 1932 by Jack Michelson and his wife Mildred. They sold Native American Indian jewelry at various tourist locations in the southwestern United States until the late 1980s. In 1972 the company name was changed to Sunbell Corp. During WWII and Korean era they made many sweetheart items and some insignia. Creased all operations in 2000.

7B

Sunbell mark

Bende & Sons Inc IOH B26
180 Autumn St
Passaic, NJ 07055

Has been in business for approximately 45 years selling various military items. They also sell via another company Michael A. Hessberg, Inc. They made embroidered insignia in the 1970's and 1980's.

Berben Insignia Co.

IOH   12B

Philadelphia, PA.
820 Fox Chase Road
Rockledge, PA
215-663-8787
www.berbeninsignia.com

Founded in 1908 by Wolf Bernstein, who was an immigrant from Russia and had been trained as a Doctor but because he could not speak English he started to sell badges instead. In 1957 the concern was purchased by Jules Gelbstein and then sold again to Herman Aion in 1962. It is currently owned by Elysee Aion and still in operation specializing in Police and Fire Badges.

Arthus Bertrand

Paris, France

http://www.arthus-bertrand.com/

Arthus-Bertrand, a maker of medals and decorations, was founded in Paris in 1803 by Claude Arthus-Bertrand, an army officer during the French Revolution. Artists who have designed for the firm include Frédéric Auguste Bartholdi (sculptor of the Statue of Liberty) and Fernand Léger. They employ nearly 300 people.

Arthus-Bertrand has had many distinguished clients including the French government. It is the official manufacturer of the French Legion of Honor and has made insignia for the Society of the Cincinnati and the Order of Lafayette.

Hallmark dating:
Arthus Bertrand Paris Depose - most widely known - early 1930s-1940
Arthus Bertrand Paris / Arthus Bertrand 46 R. de Rennes - 1950s-1960s
Arthus Bertrand (Pour Editions Atlas) - this is a modern souvenir type that has no military issue - 2000s
NOTE: Arthus-Bertrand also made badges that feature simply a small square hallmark. Some of these are original pre-WW2 issue, others are post war re-strikes.

Joe C. Bettencourt Company
San Antonio, TX. I

Mr. Bettencourt was a veteran of WWI served as a Private. It appears he went into the jewelery business after the war.

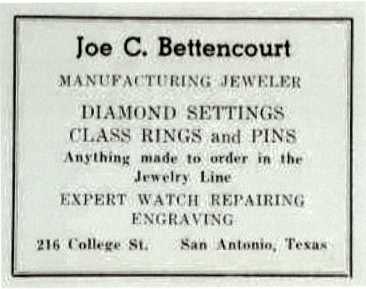

San Antonio Junior College Yearbook 1938

Beverly Craft. (palm tree logo) W
8477 W 4th St
Beverly Hills, CA
Carl Cook Veneman and T. A. Arthur
It appears they were a metal arts company founded in 1942 that produced many forms of insignia's prior to and during WWII. They also held a patent for a letter scale in 1940 and were still making scales in the 1950's. They produced many forms of sweetheart pins and charms as well.

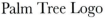

Palm Tree Logo

Beverly Craft was a rather quickly conceived and short lived operation. C. C. Veneman, was a constant inventor and metal crafter, he was hoping for a job with a large lamp company in California. It didn't work out. He was searching for other ways to make money and decided to buy some used metal crafting equipment, namely a drop hammer press, to manufacture jewelry. The drop hammer press didn't appear. What did was a lot of used manufacturing equipment. So Mr. Veneman started a used equipment supply list that he created, printed and distributed on the west coast titled aptly "The Pacific Coast Buyers Guide."

After selling the guide, he invented and patented a small cheap postal scale. Unfortunately the scale's plastic parts kept warping so what started off as a promising venture ended up being a bust.

Around 1939-1940, with war on the horizon, the enterprising Mr. Veneman decided to get into military jewelry (what we would call sweetheart pieces). Again, he could not find a more traditional drop hammer press. He was able to put a down payment on an old fifty ton embossing press. This was not the typical machinery used. It was a constantly running up and down machine that was meant to emboss a constant feed of metal. Not to press out individual pieces. Veneman found a gambling die maker who made up a couple of bracelet patterns and alphabet series of letters. He had no money for a trim die so he had to finish the pieces by hand with a drill press and hand files. The work was dangerous because of the constant motion of the embossing press. One had to quickly insert the blank or planchet into the running machine. Also, the machine would only impress one side.

Finally Veneman made enough pieces that we has able to hire a salesman who brought back thousands of orders for the bracelets. He was also able to hire a "pegleg character…a bull-necked tough guy, who I am sure, served time, and probably lost his leg in a gun fight." He apparently was a natural at the embossing press. His record according to Veneman was 3,000 coined pieces a day. Apparently with the drop hammer press usually used by the big firms in provenance or Attleboro, they could only put out 500-600 pieces a day.

Veneman opened the Beverly Craft company office on 4th street near La Cienega in Los Angeles, just around the block from the famous restaurant row. His target was selling to PX's and military stores. He eventually expanded to men's tailors and haberdashers that specialized in military uniforms "who could outfit an entire graduation class in one fitting."

As the war started and materials became short, Veneman could no longer order brass for his bracelets. Instead he got a government contract to produce military insignia like rank, branch of service and wings. This allowed him to purchase brass and sterling silver again. His business boomed, especially since he priced his material three times as high as other big companies who could not increase prices once they became fixed by the OPA.

By 1943, "the army announced that after a certain date all insignia would have to be purchased through the central Post Exchange in New York." Veneman could no longer purchase raw metal materials unless he went to the black market. Instead, he discontinued making military insignia and closed the company.

He took his profits and purchased a lovely home in Beverly Hills off Coldwater Canyon at the top of the hill. "Our five neighbors included Ginger Rogers, John Hayes Hammond and Jascha Heifetz. Naturally I joined a country club and from about ten a.m. played gin until lunch - then golf and bridge until dinner time, when our wives would join us to complete the perfect day."

Charles Cook Veneman continued to work in metal crafts the rest of his life with his sons, designing modern furniture and lighting. He is survived by grandchildren and further generations that primarily live in Spain.

Biederman Co.
Bonn, Germany
Formed May 14, 1938 and no longer in business.

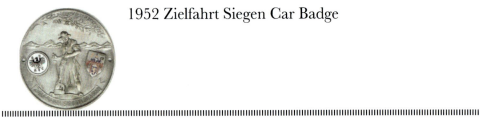

1952 Zielfahrt Siegen Car Badge

Bijou
Michael J. Pechacek
Phoenix, AZ
This hallmark was created for reproduction of WWI French Squadron pins. The company Bijou never existed.

Bippart, Griscomb and Osborn
2-8 Garden St
Newark, NJ

Founded in 1886 by Achill Bippart as Bipprt & Co. Benjamin F. Griscom joined the company in 1893. Bennet Osborn, Jr., became a member of the company in 1897. They were a major manufacture that included fine gold jewelery, and a full line of mourning and platinum jewelery. In the early 1930's they were acquired by Krementz and Company. It does not appear they manufacturer military insignia but did make sweetheart items. It is also possible that the shown they only supplied the clasp.

Wallace Bishop Co.
Brisbane, Australia

Founded in 1917 by Mr. Wallace Bishop and currently still in business owned by the same family operating a jewelry store chain of 57 units. During World War II, Wallace Bishop was appointed the official enamel badge maker for the Australian Defense Department, producing 27,000 badges.

B.J. Co. (by Orber). I
It is believed this was an off shoot of Orber but nothing is known.

V. H. Blackinton Company   IOH B24
Attleboro Falls, MA (VHB). I, W

Founded in 1852 under the leadership of Virgil Blackinton in Attleboro Falls, Massachusetts. They moved into military insignia as a result of commissions during the Civil War. They are now in business making police and fire badges. They do make wings and other insignia but not for the military at this time.

Black, Starr & Frost, Ltd

Founded in 1810 in Savannah, GA as Marquand & Co and in 1839 became Bell, Thompkins & Black. In 1851 the name changed to Ball, Black & Co. which lasted until 1876 when they became Black, Starr & Frost. In 1929 they merged with Gorham Co and the name became Black, Starr & Frost-Gorham until 1940 when they dropped the Frost part of the name until 1962 when they went to the name above. In 1966 they no longer were part of the Gorham family and no longer manufacture products. They made insignia prior to the Civil War and in WWI.

Hallmark from the WWI era.

Blumberg Bros
276 Fifth Ave
New York, NY.
Cage Code: 93824
Formed in 1906 by Max and Julius Blumberg.
Incorporated July 24, 1946.

BB
N.Y.C.

They would place a B and the year on the back of patches.

Bond
These wings while hallmarked Bond appear to have been manufactured by Blackinton. No other information is known about this company. It appears they were just a seller of insignia.

M.S. Bowman
New York, NY.

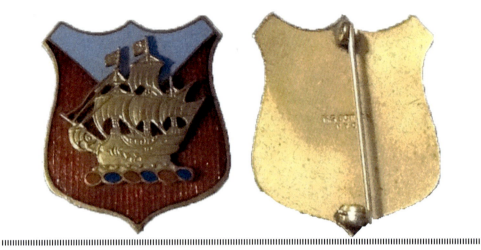

Branded Emblem Co. IOH B28
7920 Foster
Overland Park, KS 66204
Founded in 1969 currently supplying law enforcement professionals with embroidered emblems and enamel pins.

Braxmar N.Y.
Charles Braxmar was a jeweler. In 1879 he founded a business making badges for fire, police and fraternal organizations. Incorporated in March 1914, the C. G. Braxmar Company became one of the principle supplier of such emblems throughout the northeast and eventually the country. Based in New York City, the company was family-owned until 2000 when it was sold to the Blackinton Company of Attleboro Falls, Massachusetts.

Spanish American War item

Believed to be 1880's

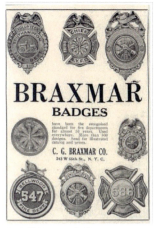
242 West 55th Street
New York, NY
1927

216 E 45th Street
New York, 17 NY
1952

1920's to 1940's

G. Bregonzio
Via Brioschi 34
Milano, Italy

German Insignia during WWII

Gustav Brehmer
Germany. I

The company of Gustav Brehmer was founded in 1871 in the town of Markneukirchen in Saxony and became one of the premier manufacturers of war badges during the Third Reich. Interestingly, Karl Wurster, owner of another major war badge manufacturer during the Third Reich began his career working for Brehmer until he eventually opened his own factory some 100 meters from Brehmer after leaving in 1912. The craftsmen at Brehmer produced some of the highest quality badges for the Luftwaffe and Heer including the numbered Panzer Assault Badge (PAB) and numbered General Assault Badge (GAB), but was perhaps most well-known for their stunning Luftwaffe Flak Badges. It appears they continued production of commercial and US military insignia after the war.

Hitler Youth Badge RZM M1/101

Post War

Brooks Awards & Medals   IOH B35
4140 Austine Blvd
Island Park, NY 11558
513-271-4858
Founded in 2003, but currently is a jobber of insignia and badges.

Broy Co Mfg & Sales Co   IOH B34
1701 Creek Dr
West Bend, WI 53095
718-786-7888
They were in business in the 1990's but no other information is known.

BS & T Corp.   IOH B30
262 Broadway
North Attleboro, MA
410-664-2800
No information on this business.

Buerge
Germany I
No information on this concern.

Fritz Buttner & Sohn
Aschaffenburg, Würzburger Str. 32
Germany.

This insignia was made in the mid to late 1950's

58

J.B. Caco
No information on this concern

Unknown 5B

C&C Metal Products   IOH C34
456 Nordhoff Place
Englewood, NJ 07631
201-854-0388

Founded in 1914, they are a major manufacturer of buttons and jewelry findings. The buttons are found on many uniforms, they have 3000 button designs and the pin backs on many US Insignia. Still in operation.

CAPA
Bruxelles (Belgian)
No information has been found on this company. The badges found would indicate they made insignia shortly after WWII.

C & P Embroidery Co., Inc.   IOH C27
6602 Smith Ave
North Bergen, NJ 07047
201-854-0388
Currently Authorized by IOH but has been reported as closed.

Cartier
Paris France

Cartier jewelry can trace back to Louis Francois Cartier a descendant of Jacques Cartier, a French explorer who first sailed up the St. Lawrence River in 1535. In 1859 Louis Philippe Carter open the first jewelry shop in Paris and in 1909 Pierre Cartier open one in New York City. Cartier never officially made US insignia but had been called upon by US soldiers in WWI in France to made items for them such as Aero Squadron badges. In WWII they gave office space to Charles de Gaulle's in their London building which served as the first HQ of the free French forces. Cartier made Free French insignia. They may have made insignia on a special order basis.

Cartier is considered one of the most prestigious jewelry houses in the world. Because of the French hallmarking system WWI items not made out of precious metals may not any markings.

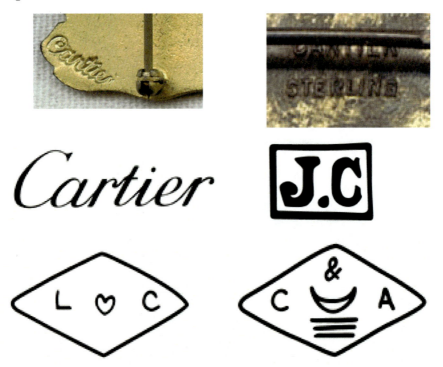

Personal Note: For a number of years the author was a supplier to Cartier in the design and production of sterling silver sculptures. For XIII (1980) Olympic Winter Games we were asked to design a Sterling Raccoon with five rings in his tail and mount it on a mineral specimen from the United States looking like snow. We selected Celestite which in small crystals looks like power blue snow. 250 of these were created. Another highlight was placement in their Christmas catalog of a sterling sculpture of an old New York street vendor with his push wagon selling vegetables and fruit made of semi-precious stones. We were awarded a Cartier hallmark steel stamp to use on products for them.

Carolina Emblems Co   IOH C28
PO BOX 368
Campobello, SC 29322
714-981-9333
Founded in 1977 making patches for Boy Scouts, corporate and military. They are still in business.

Carolina Service Co.   IOH C25
Fayetteville, NC. I
No information on this company.

S.D. Childs & Co.
Chicago, IL. I
Established in 1821 by Shubael D. Childs. In 1839 they advertised that were engravers and by 1860 claimed to be the largest engravers west of New York City. They were known for their engraving and coins and tokens. Chicago Police badges and GAR badges. It is not known when the company ceased to exist.

Cindarn Plastics Inc   IOH C26
1532 Wesst Baltimore St
Baltimore, MD 21223
508-695-6215
Cage Code 5A289
Founded in 1982 and still in operation.

Citco I
No information on this supplier.

CKS
Seoul, South Korea. I
Manufacturer of US Army DIs in the early 1950's.

Classic Medallics, Inc.   IOH   C31   Non-certified CM
520 S Fulton Ave
Mt Vernon, NY 10550
800-221-1348
http://classic-medallics.com/

Started in 1940 as a manufacturer of religious jewelry under the name of Frederick Singer & Sons. The company soon after became a dominant player in the religious gift industry. In the late 1950's, the Singer family saw a golden opportunity to bring it's manufacturing and design experience to the rapidly growing awards industry, which at that time was just beginning to adopt production methods to mass-produce awards. Classic Medallics quickly became one of the leaders and innovators in developing a wide variety of quality metallic products, mass-produced at affordable prices. Currently authorized to manufacture medals and Distinctive Unit Insignias.

CM GI Hallmark

Clayton
Chicago, IL. I
No information on this supplier

Clover Embroidery Works   IOH C21
No information on this company.

College Shops
Attleboro, MA. I
Items form the early 1900's have been found but no additional information.

Colonial Promotions   IOH C29
No information on this company.

Colorado Stitchery   IOH C33
770-101 Wooten Rd
Colorado Springs, CO
No information on this company.

Columbia Button & Nailhead Corp.   IOH C24
306-316 Stagg St.
Brooklyn, NY 11206
(718) 386-3414
Cage Code 5A870

D. George Collins, Ltd.
118 Newgate St, London EC 1

Established in 1891 as a manufacturer of cutlery, medals, trophies and badges. It is believed this is a fake production of the paratrooper badge but bears a Collins hallmark. It is not know it they made any other US insignia, they did make British Medals.

Cooper Industries   IOH C30
554 North Central Ave
Upland, CA 91786

In addition to any insignia they manufactured M-16 magazine that were found to be defective.

Coro (Cohn & Rosenberger)   IOH 12C
New York, NY/Providence, RI.   I, M, W

Coro jewelry, Cohn & Rosenberger, was founded in New York by Emanuel Cohn & Carl Rosenberger in 1901/1902 & incorporated in 1913. A factory was established in Providence, RI in 1911.

Cohn died in 1910, but the name remained Cohn & Rosenberger. The corporate name "Coro" was adopted in 1943. Rosenberger died in 1957, & his son Gerald, who succeeded him, died in 1967.

In 1969 the family sold 51% of the Coro stock to Richton, Intl. Corp., and the rest in 1970. Richton also owned the Oscar de la Renta brand. By 1979 all the Coro companies, were bankrupt and sold to a South American company in 1992 which also went bankrupt.

Cover Stitches   IOH C35
567 52Nd St
West New York, NY 07093
Sales of uniforms for schools and T-shirts. Currently in business.

Craftens Inc.
Chicago, IL. I
No information has been found on this supplier.

Creative Modeling & Die Mfg Co.   IOH C32
417 John Dietsch Blvd
North Attleboro, MA
508-336-6433
Founded in 1968 and has made military challenge coins and other awards. Still in business.

Creed Jewelry
Attleboro Massachusetts

Founded in 1946 by William Creed with their primary business centered around Catholic rosaries, the Creed company also made many high quality charms during the period. Generally they are a medallion or cross style and have a design on the front and either a religious design or inspirational message on the back. In 1989 the Creed Company was sold but still remained in business in Wrentham MA. In 2011 Creed was acquired by Christian Brands, located in Phoenix Arizona. They made Christian military medallion that never were official or authorized.

 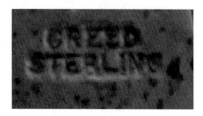

Crest-Craft Co.

IOH   14C, 23C, C23

3860 Virginia Ave
Cincinnati, OH 45227
(513) 271-4858   http://crestcraft.com

Crest-Craft was founded in 1946 by a decorated WWII veteran. The company was initially formed with the single purpose of recognizing the heroic accomplishments of our military servicemen and women. Today they continue to service all branches of our Military, worldwide. Crest-Craft is a market leader in the design, development and production of custom emblematic awards and recognition products. In 2015 they renewed their IOH Hallmark and manufactured a 75th Anniversary Paratrooper badge under C-23.

Crisalli

P.O. Box 7277
Northridge, CA 91327
(818) 368-6230

FAX: (805) 520-7391

http://crisalli.com/

Criisalli was founded in 1951. In 1978 they started to make cast insignia in Sterling silver, 14K white or yellow gold. Custom work. They do not have an IOH number.

Daniel Low & Co.
Washiington St
Salem MA

Founded in 1867 by Daniel Low as a jewelry store in Salem. In 1887 they adopted the concept of souvenir spoons with his son Seth having designed the Witch spoon as a souvenir of Salem know for its witches of the 1600's. In 1893 they started a mail order business and a boom in various spoons and silver gifts the "Daniel Yearbook" grew to over 200 pages. In 1896 Seth became a partner and in 1907 the name was incorporated. In 1911 Daniel passed away and Seth took over the business. Later the company was run by Seth's widow Florence until the mid-1950s. In 1955, Bill Follett bought and ran the company until it was sold, along with the building in 1994. The only know item made for the military is the Flying Witch squadron pin for the 345th Aero Squadron of WWI.

Danecraft, Inc.
One Baker St
Providence, RI   02905
401.941.7700   www.danecraft.com

Founded by Victor Primavera, Sr. in 1934 and was the head of the company until his death in February 1977. It appears they only made a few items during WWII and in most cases they are stamped with a Pat number or Pat Pend. as part of their hallmarked. A number of their items such as the CAA set shown here did not have their hallmark on them. They were well known for non-military intricate and high quality sterling silver charms, bracelets, necklaces, earrings and pendants.

ARTIFACT: Nearly identical to the more commonly seen CPT Enlisted Reserve (Program Graduation) wing, this War Training Service flight school graduation wing made by Danecraft dates from early WWII after the organizational name change (to War Training Service), but before the issuance of the wing was discontinued, circa 1942. This wing was made taking the more commonly seen wing (but with a more rare style of Danecraft Maker Mark!) and having the area where CPT (For Civilian Pilot Training) planed off, and soldering in a panel with the initials of the CPT successor: War Training Service (or WTS) in its place. It is extremely well done, and hard to tell if a quantity of these wings were sent to a jeweler for the modification after the 1942 organizational change, or if the wings were sent back to Danecraft for the modification. In any event, the wing is extremely rare, as it is the only one I have seen, and when conferring with collectors of WWII Pilot Training, I have found none who have encountered one before.

Freeman Daughaday Co.
Chartley Village, Norton, MA through 1946, then Providence, RI

Founded in 1861 by William Sturdy. it later became Sturdy & Marcy and then became Freeman & Daughaday Co. It is not know when they ceased being in business.
In 1943 they had an Army contract to manufacture Purple Hearts. These were not numbered.

Davorn Industries
119 West 42nd St
New York, NY 10011

Primary focus of their business was costume jewelry.

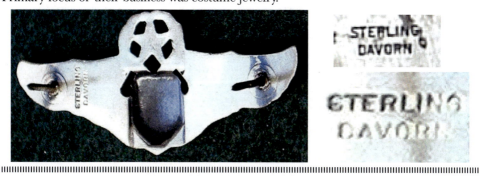

DAWN - McCarthy & Hamrick
It is believed this company was sales only and purchased from others and applied this hallmark. The DAWN OF TEXAS hallmark was used by this company. It is possible they just used DAWN. The wing that is shown was manufactured by Angelo Dimaria, Inc.

Davidson & Sons Jewelry Company Inc.
20 West 47th St
New York, NY 10036

Founded in 1932 and creased operations in 2012. Their trademark (HENDA) expired in 2004. It is believed during WWII they may have made some insignia of sweetheart jewelry.

The Dawson Company
Cleveland, OH
Several companies have this name but none related to military.

Delancy School of Marketing   IOH D24
No information on this concern

Denazio
Corizia, Italy. I
No information on this supplier.

Denmark's Military Equipment Corp.
IOH 6D, D22

New York/Astoria, NY. (Best Embroidery Company) (Best Emblem Company)
They had an affiliate Eveready Embroidery, Inc. They moved to Jersey City and shortly after the move they went out of business in 2007. In 1995 they were charged with price fixing on contracts with Army Air Force Exchange Service.
They were also known for suppling Museum Gift Shops in the 80's and 90's with reproduction WWII wings and insignia

A.J. Dennison, Riverside, RI.   IOH 5D, D23

1 East St, Riverside, RI 02915
(401) 433-3232
http://www.ajdennison.com

A. J. Dennison was founded in 1920 in the production high quality, custom emblematic jewelry. This is the style of manufacturing that would have been ideal for making DIs. They are still in business.

Deschler & Sohn
Munich, Germany. I

1894 Pre WWII

Three above WWII

1964

1967

Designer Tool & Die   IOH   D27
49 Industrial Ct
Seekonk, MA 02771   914-425-2245

Metal Stamping company founded in 1984 and went out of business in 2009.

Detail Manufacturing Co Inc.   IOH   D26
No information on this company.

Diana's Flags & Guidons   IOH   D28
2501 S.W.S. Young Drive Ste 207
Killeen, TX 76542
800-682-5155

Supplier of flags and military name tags.

Dieges & Clust
New York & Providence RI, I, M

Dieges & Clust were jewellers established in New York in 1898 by Col. Charles J. Dieges (b. Oct. 26, 1865-d. Sept. 14, 1953) and Prosper Clust. They made the Spanish American War Medal, 1904 Olympic Medal, US Medal of Honor and were the second manufacturer of Eagle Scout Medal having made approximately 1640 medals between 1916 and 1920. They made baseball pins and medals and educational award medals. They were also known for making the Heisman Trophy from its inception in 1935 through late 1979 In 1979 the company was sold to Herff Jones.

WWII Command Pilot
John Vargas Collection

Angelo Di Maria, Inc.
395 Admiral St.
Providence, RI 20940

Founded in 1971 they were a metal stamping company to the trade. They made jewelry and insignia parts for other companies including insignia for N.S. Meyer. It is believed they went out of business in the 2005 time period. See photo with Dawn listing page 69.

Discovery Marketing & Design   IOH   D29
90 Middle Street
Pawtucket, RI 02860
401-725-1404

Founded in 1982 by David L Stabb specializing in men's and women's jewelry, gifts and accessories and have developed custom and proprietary engraving and finishing techniques available only in our U.S. manufacturing facility. Authorized to manufacture medals.

Dibb Jewelers aka Walter Dibb & Sons
1022 First National Bldg
San Diego, CA

Founded by Walter Dibb. He arrived in San Diego in 1904 from Toronto, Canada. It is not know when the company starting in business and some records show it was still in business as late as 1946. It is believed they only made this one military insignia during WWI.

Diversified Metal Crafters Inc.   IOH   D30
4 Carol Dr
Lincoln, RI 02865
401-305-7700

Manufacturer of custom emblematic jewelry and quality metal products.

Diversified Products Inc.   IOH   D25
106 Jospital St
Providence, RI 02903
414-354-7800

No information on this business.

Dobbins. I
No information is known about this supplier.

Dodge Inc.
Chicago, IL. I

Dodge & Asher
Chicago, IL

1930 hallamrk

Dodge Trophy Co.
Los Angeles, CA.
They used to make the Oscars until 1983 when they went out of business.

Founded by Ray E. Dodge originally as Dodge Co of Chicago, IL and moved to Los Angeles in 1930 and changed its name to Dodge Trophy Co. They became very well known when they began making the Oscars in association with the Southern California Trophy Co. The company began manufacturing Emmy's for the television industry in 1949. Dodge Inc. also manufactured Rose Bowl and Orange Bowl football trophies. Mr. Dodge passed away in 1985.

Dohmer
Germany (D1) I

No information on this supplier.

Dommers
Germany. I

No information on this supplier.

A.H. Dondero
IOH   D2, D21

Washington, DC

Current address
P.O. Box 59
Brownsburg, Virginia 24415
Phone: 540.348.6753 / Fax: 540.348.6293
Email: pete@dondero.com
Web site: http://www.dondero.com

Col. A. H. Dondero founded the company in 1922. He was a retired Quartermaster officer and recognized the need for quality uniforms. In the early 1970's they changed direction to become a recognition awards company and by 1976 they totally switched. In 1979 Sue and Pete Hecht purchased the company and the name changed to Dondero, Inc from A.H. Dondero, Inc. and moved from Washington to Brownsburg, VA.

WWII

Koren era to 1954

1954-1965

Post 1965

Donner
Elberfeld, Germany

United States Army 368th Engineer Battalion DI post war.

N.C. Dorrety 1
Dorrety of Boston
387 Washington St
Boston MA

Dorest Company
3rd & Vine St
Cincinnati, OH
Modern- Dorst Jewelry and Mfg. Co
2100 Reading Rd
Cincinati OH 45202-1418
CAGE 8N711

Founded in 1888 by Jacob Dorst and Joseph Jonas as Jonas, Dorst & Co. The name changed after Mr. Jonas died in the early 1900's. In the 1940's it became known as Dorst Jewelry Co. In 1983 the business was acquired by the brothers, William and Douglas Turnbull and in 1995 the company was renamed as The John Gray Awards Company.

DRAGO
France

Drago 25 R. Beranger Paris Depose (III)- often 1936-1940
Drago Depose / Drago Paris Nice (Depose) - a bit more flexible - 1944-1947
Drago 43 R. Olivier Metra - immediate postwar (colonial) - 1947-1952
Drago 3. R. de Romainville Paris - 1952-1960
Drago Paris - most common and longest running marking - generally used from 1960-1990
Drago Marne la Vallee 1990 -1995

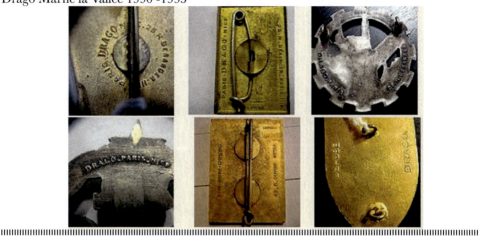

E. A. Dreher & Son
42 Walnut St
Newark NJ
Established in the early 1900's the firm specialized in 14kt gold and platinum jewelry.

Durocharm
New York City. I
Unknown dates in business but have found school pins from the early 1950's. Made insignia, DIs and sweetheart items during WWII.

Dan S. Dunham
San Antonio, TX
He was born in 1877 and died in 1955. Operated a very successful jewelry store and business in San Antonio.

C. B. Dyer
Insignia Manufacturer. No information is known.

Eagle Regalia Co.   IOH   E24
115 Nassau St
New York
Current:
747 Chestnut Ridge Road
Chestnut Ridge, NY 10977
Phone: 845-425-2245
www.eagleregalia.com

Founded in New York City in 1910, Eagle Regalia Company's origins include manufacturing in three product areas: banners and flags, emblematic jewelry and badges, and awards of various types crafted in metal and wood.

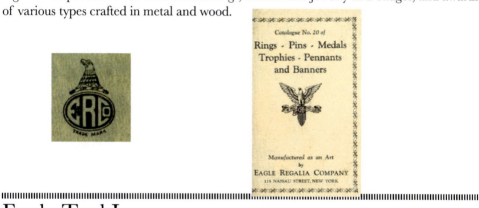

Eagle Tool Inc.   IOH   E35
430 Kinsley Avenue
Providence RI 02909
(401)421-5105
Founded in 1946 as a metal stamping company and still in operation.

S.E. Eby
Philadelphia, PA. I, M, W

The company was founded in 1935 as a maker of police and fire badges in sterling silver it is not known when it creased to exist but appears to have still been in business in the early 1950's. On May 13, 1943 the name was registered in Pennsylvania.

Ebsco Industries, Inc.   IOH E28
Birmingham, AL. I

Founded in the 1930's by Elton B. Stephens to sell magazine subscriptions. Is a conglomerate of many information and other companies. One of which is Military Service Company and another is Vulcan Products.

Eiseman-Ludmar Co, Inc.   IOH E31
56 Bethpage Dr
Hicksville, NY 11801
516-932-6330

http://www.elcaccessories.com

Hand Embroidered Bullion. Founded in 1955 by Abraham Duke Eiseman and his brother-in-law Joseph Ludmar and still in operation as a uniform accessory company.

Eisenstadt Jewelry Co.
Eisenstadt Manufacturing Co.
M Eisenstadt Mfg. Co
Founded around 1853 by Michael G. Eisenstadt
1409 Washington St
St.Louis, MO 63103

Eisenstadt had a number of Trademarks all of which expired in the 1980's when they went out of business. Some of their WWI dies were kept by employees and re-strikes came on the market as a result.

1909 Ad

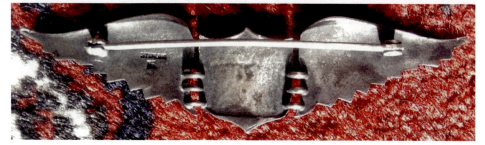

Elco Embroidery Works   IOH E22
No information on this company.

Elden Industries   IOH E32
425 Station St
Cranston, RI. 02910
(401) 467-7733
Founded in 1987 as a manufacturer of Jewelry, Watches, Precious Stones, and Precious Metals.

Elwyn Industries Inc.   IOH E29
Elwyn, PA.
No information on this company.

Emblem and Badge Co.   IOH E21
28 Sunnyside Av
Johnston, RI , 02919
401-331-5444
Established in 1932 as a small maker of ribbons, emblems, & insignia in Providence RI. Still in business as an awards company with retail outlets. Current address shown.

Emblemcraft Ltd   IOH E25
New York, NY. I
Was registered with the State of New York on February 15, 1966 with offices in Freeport NY. On June 23, 1993 the company was dissolved.
Can only find that they manufactured DIs and used two different hallmarks.

Emblem Supply Co. Inc.   IOH 1E, E23
Central Falls, RI

Emblematic Trades, Inc.
New York, NY

Hallmarks are shown from the back of warrant officer insignia and master paratrooper from early 1950's. No additional information is known about this company.

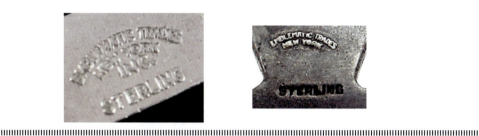

Empire State Metal Products
101-10 Jamaica Ave
Richmond Hill, NY 11418
718-847-1617

Currently listed as an approved metals manufacturer but not assigned an IOH number.

Erffmeyer & Son, Inc.   AKA Esco   IOH E-27
5300 W. Clinton Ave
Milwaukee, WI 53223
414-354-7800
www.escoinc.com

In 1934, The Erffmeyer & Son Company was established in downtown Milwaukee, in the Plankinton Building. Chet Erffmeyer, a young salesman for the Bundy and Upmeyer Company, a jewelry manufacturing and card making business, purchased and took over the emblematic division, reestablishing it as Erffmeyer & Son Company, Inc. (ESCO). Chet Erffmeyer, with his wife Lillian alongside him, worked to produce emblematic jewelry and awards for various fraternal and religious groups nationwide and for local organizations and companies in the Milwaukee area. In 1951 Chet passed away and his son Robert took over and not only ran the company but also became a Major General in the US Army. Still family owned. Authorized for Medals and Distinctive Unit Insignias.

Eveready Embroidery Inc.   IOH E26
235 Orient Ave
Jersey City, NJ 07305
Founded in 2008 as a Schiffli Machine Embroidery Company. However it appears they may no longer be in business.

Everson Ross Co.   IOH E30
56 Church St
Spring Valley, NY 10977
913-888-8880
Was a leading badge manufacturer established in 1897 and is now part of Smith & Warren.

 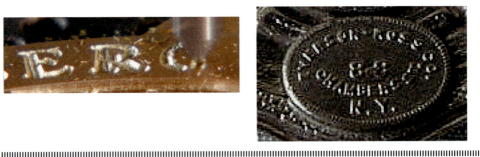

Fawn Industries Inc.   IOH F24
Route 851
New Park, PA 17352
703-335-9292
Established in 1983 by H.William Clarius and does custom embroidery. Still in operation.

FBF Industries Inc.   IOH F26
1145 Industrial Blvd
Southampton, PA 18966
800-647-6188
FBF Tool and Die was founded in Philadelphia in 1943 as a stamping tool builder. In 1976, the company changed its name to FBF Industries and moved to its current location. In 1994 the name was once again changed to FBF Inc. They are a metal stamping company and many other metal related work such as assembly and welding of parts.

Finishing Touch Embroideries   IOH F25
6015 Broadway
West New York, NY 07093
Founded in 1986. Does not appear to be in business.

Firmin & Sons
London, England.

Established in 1677 with origins dating back to before the reign of Charles II, Firmin & Sons is one of the longest established companies in the United Kingdom. Originally based in the City of London, the Company moved to Birmingham, the manufacturing heartland of the UK, in the late 19 th Century.

Firmin & Sons Limited.
Firmin House,
82-86 New Town Row,
Birmingham , B6 4HU

FIX
France

Was founded in the early 19th century by Francois Savard who worked in the Marais district. His process used an unusually thick layer of 18 ct or 14 ct gold foil over brass to form jewelery which would withstand long term wear and be easily mistaken for real gold. In 1893 son Auguste Savard who took over the company and registered the trademark FIX. At one point they had 300 employees. They made WWI Eagles that were worn by many French pilots and also made DI type insignia for US Aero Squadrons. The last record of the company was in the early 1970's, with the business in the town of Saint Amand Montrand run by Jean Savard who was the grandson of the founder.

Fontana Rehabilitation Workshop
(aka Industrial Support Systems)
8608 Live Oak Ave
Fontana, CA, 92335 United States
(909) 428-3833
Cage Code OVEZ2

Established in 1964 as a workshop for students in the Fontana School District with disabilities. In 1974 they changed their name to Industrial Support Systems. They have contracts with the federal government to package and assemble military badges. It is doubtful they manufactured any badges.

Bruce Fox Inc.   IOH   F27
1909 McDonald Ln
New Albany, IN 47151

Founded in 1938 by Bruce Fox who was a trained commercial artist. They curenly design and manufacture custom designed award plaques and trophies for the corporate world.

Gustave Fox Co.
411-13 Race St
Cincinnati, OH. I, W

When Gustave Fox was 14 years old when he started the company in 1869 as a jeweler doing repairs, by 1900 25 people were employed doing repairs, special orders and started to do emblem work. The company seemed to vanish in 1922 with its last listing in the Jeweler Circular, but during WWII wings appeared with the Fox hallmark. Also some emblem work as shown below. Some wings were sterling and some were brass silver plated without the sterling mark, just the F in the circle with the X in the background.

 Hallmark WWII

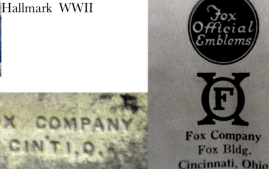

Fox Company
Fox Bldg.
Cincinnati, Ohio

WWII Era Emblem with hallmark from reverse.

Fox Military Equipment Co.
Hinsdale, IL / Clarendon Hills, IL

Founded by Alan Beckman who was a manufacturer of reproduction insignia and an importer of overseas military insignia. When NS Meyer went out of business he obtained the many of the Meyer dies and manufactured re-strikes. The business was closed in 2013.

P.J. Friedel
Philadelphia, PA

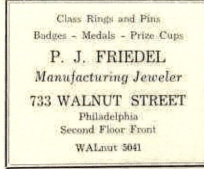 Ad from 1941

Frielich Brothers

IOH F21N

New York, NY
Very little information on this company. They manufactured military hats.

August C. Frank Co.

Philadelphia, PA M

Founded August C. Frank Company, Philadelphia, 1894. He was probably the only engraver for the firm in early years, later he accepted dies engraved by others that his firm would strike. After he died the firm was operated by his sons but ultimately sold to Medallic Art Company, 15 September 1972.

Frank Brothers

IOH 2F

San Antonio, TX. I

Frank Bros. (Gerson, Emil, and Sol Frank), established in 1868. Known for its fine men's clothing, it was sold in 1963 and ceased operations in 1995

Lorioli Fratelli
Milano, Italy. I

Unable to find examples of US Insignia made by this company.

1940 Catalog

Thomas Frattorinin
Regent Street Works
Birmingham, West Midlands B1 3HQ
United Kingdom
www.fattorini.co.uk   Tel:+44 121 236 1307

The company was founded in 1827 by Antonio Fattorini an Italian speaking immigrant who settled in Yorkshire where he established a number of retail outlets specializing in jewelry, watches and fancy goods including barometers. Made WWII US Insignia.

Hallmark adopted in 1934

John Frick Jewelry Co.
New York. I

Founded in the 1890's as a maker of corp badges and pins for the Spanish American war by John Frick, F W Moesel and Alex Arnold.

Fulford Mfg. Co. IOH F22
65 Tripps Lane
East Providence, RI 02915
401-431-2000

The business was founded in the 1880's by Harry Fulford, an English toolmaker who crossed the Atlantic looking for a better life. It was incorporated in 1890 and grew to employ 24 toolmakers and over 400 employees. In 1985 the business was sold to Anthony Hart. Today Fulford Manufacturing has two major business sectors. One sector provides precision stamped and formed parts to the automotive and other OEM industries. The other sector, Gold 'N' Things, provides product almost exclusively to the jewelry industry.

Samual Gallini IOH G29N
300 East 33rd St
New York, NY 10016

No information on this business.

Gamber Products Co. Inc. IOH G30
45 Fullerton Rd
Warwick, RI 02886
401-732-5832

Founded in 1946. Current listing is for machine shop and machine repairs.

J.R. Gaunt & Son
London, Birmingham, England/New York, NY.

Gaunt was established in 1733, some claim they started in 1750, and were well know for its insignia to the British military worldwide. Somewhere around 1925 the name changed to J R Gaunts and Sons. Around 1870 to the 1970s Gaunt manufactured Uniform Buttons as well as swords, badges. In 1991 they were purchased by Firmin and Sons. In 2010 the Company trademark was re-established in the UK by the Gaunt family.

Gemsco
(General Embroidery and Military Supply Company)

USMC Quartermaster ID 220, 298, IOH G2, G22

262 Quarry Road
Milford, CT 06460-8504

They were founded in 1881 in New York City. The last know listing for the company was 1965 which would explain the G-22 hallmark.

Special Note: For many years this company has been mis-ID it was believed that Gemsco stood for General Merchandising Company. Because the "Internet" never forgets it may take years before all the charts and listings get corrected.

"Our Navy" magazine June 1921, August 1921

General Display Co.
MasterCraft Awards

IOH G-25

10390 Central Park Dr
Manassas, VA 20110
703-335-9292

www.generaldisplaycompany.com

MasterCraft Awards and General Display Company is a small, veteran-owned business that has served the Washington Metropolitan area and beyond since 1967. Known for making wooden seals from 3 to 72 inches in size.

General Insignia Corp. I
626 Whittier St
Bronx, NY

It is believed they were a post WWII company but it appears they did not last long.

(Note: care should be taken not to confuse this maker with The Institute of Heraldry's certification mark "GI"(Government Issue), which is unrelated)

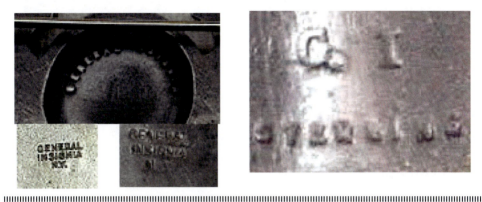

General Products Company, Inc.
Providence, RI.

There is a great deal of confusion between General Products and Charles Polk. Both appeared to use a very similar hallmark. However General Products was listed as Metals manufacturer and Charles Polk as an insignia manufacturer.

General Products
Contental Falls, RI,
Providence, RI
Manufacturer of medals.

George & Sidney's Brass Shop
Taipei, Taiwan (G&S Co). I
No information has been found.

Gerocastelli (Lorioli Castelli?)
Italy. I

George S. Gethen Co.
Philadelphia, PA. I
Formed in 1913 and incorporated in July 1919 by George S Gethen and Harry S Sage. It appears they were in business prior as early as 1886 as swords they made have appeared from the Spanish American War era. They were in the uniform business until around 1929.

GGFXA See S.E. Eby Co.

GIBCO
Several Companies have this name so we were not able to determine details.

GJM Mfg. Inc.   IOH   G32
453 South Main St
Attleboro, MA 02703
(508) 222-9322
Is listed as a wire form manufacturer that was founded in 1977.

Gleason-Wallace
683 Broadway
Albany, NY.
From school yearbook ads it appears this company was in business in the 1930's. The DI shown is pre-war 156 Field Artillery.

Goodwear Fabrics
Made clothing under government contracts during WWII and may have made some insignia. They made A-2 jackets, sweaters, Pilot and Aerial Gunner wings.
Not to be confused with another company that was founded in 1983 making sweatshirts and sports apparel with the exact same name. Nor with the tire maker.

Gordon's Fort Meade

IOH 13G, G18

Odenton, MD.
Military Manufacturers of Maryland (by Gordon's Fort Meade)
Products were sold under two names as listed above.

Gordon B. Miller & Co.
Miller Jewelry Company
Cincinnati, OH

The company started as the Miller Jewelry Company makers of fraternal jewelry. In 1903 an ad for the company shows these products. Some time between 1931 and 1943 the name changed to the Gordon B. Miller & Co. In 1990 the company was purchased by Jostens, Inc. In the Josten information it cites Gorden Miller as the oldest the oldest recognition products company in North America.

Graco Awards, Inc.

IOH G27

723 S Cherry Street
Tomball, TX 77375-6620
800-421-0227
www.gracoind.com   Cage No 6Y663

Founded in 1981. In 2011 this company was purchased by Northwest Territory Mint. Graco continues to operate as a division. They manufacture many of the US Government medals including the current Medal of Honor.

M.M. Graham
Los Angeles, CA I
No information on this supplier.

Grannat Brothers
San Francisco, CA.
Also spelled with one N - Granat
Leo and Joseph I Gtannat started a jewelry and repair shop is 1905 in Stockton, CA. Around 1915 they moved to San Francisco and expanded their operations to wholesale diamond rings nationwide. In 1971 their retail operation was sold to Zale Jewelry Co. Their manufacturing operation was sold to another unknown concern.

1947 Trademark 71542921

Great American Weaving Corp   IOH G31
20 North Front Street
Bally, PA 19503
610-845-9200

http://www.greatamericanweaving.com

Great American Weaving Corporation founded in 2000 and located in Bally, Pennsylvania is a narrow woven fabrics manufacturer. Fabrics include woven tapes, ribbons, belts, webbings, and other specialty woven fabrics. They weave commercial and military specification webbings, including Class I shuttle loom webbing.

They are listed because they manufacture most if the woven belts used by the military today. They also make ribbons used on metals.

The Greenduck Corp.   IOH G26
Chicago, IL. Now Hernando, MS

The Greenduck Metal Stamping Company was founded in 1909 by George G. Greenburg and Harvey Ducgheisel. Say the first syllable of each of their last names and you get the company name. They were a metal stamping company but also made political buttons and license plates. As well as coins. In 1962 the ownership changed and they moved from Chicago to Hernando, Mississippi. They changed ownership again and by 2004 went out of business.

Three Union marks and Greenduck Co.

The Green Company   IOH   6G, G24
Kansas City, MO. I
15550 W. 109th Street
Lenexa, KS 66219
913-888-8880

http://www.thegreencompany.com

Founded in 1885, currently specializes in award and recognition products. Also known as KC Green.

Ira Greene Co.   IOH   3G, G3, G23
177 GEORGIA AVE
PROVIDENCE, RI 02905
800-663-7487
www.iragreen.com

Founded in 1943 as a contract manufacturer of military insignia, Ira Green, Inc. (IGI) has expanded into a full service manufacturer and distributor of nearly 40,000 unique items for the military.

The Gross Organization   IOH   G28
6805 Benito Ct
Fort Worth, TX 76126
540-261-1546
No information on this business.

Guérault
119 rue St Denis
Paris France
No information on this business.

AT Gunner & Co.
Attleboro, MA

Started manufacture in 1920 mainly in hollowware and flatware.
Many have incorrectly cited this wing as military but it actually was made for Goodyear-Zepplin Co for their Airship Captains.

Gus Manufacturing Co.
Eighth and Carpenter Streets
Philadelphia, PA

The business was founded around 1914 by Augustine "Gus" Carosiello, and owned by him until it closed in 1970. Then re-opend and finally closed in 1990 when he died in an auto accident. He mainly did castings and not die struck items. Mainly jewelry.

V. Haacke & Co.
Pforzheim, Germany. I

Irvin H. Hahn Company   IOH 1H, H22
1830R Worcester Street
Baltimore, MD 21230
(410) 685-6337
http://www.irvinhahn.com

This company was founded in 1898 by Joseph Henry Ferdinand Hahn and is still in existence as a manufacturer of police and fire badges. Hanco/rooster logo.

Hallmark Emblems Inc   IOH H-27
2401 Tampa Street
Tampa FL 33602
800-237-2567

Founded approximately 50 years ago is a manufacturer of embroidered emblems under government contracts.

Haltom Jewelers
317 Main St
Fort Worth, TX.
817-336-4051

Founded in 1893 by the Haltom family. Still in business as fine jewelers. It is believed they only made items for military wear during WWI.

Walter E. Hayward Company, Inc.

20 Capron St
(AKA- C. E. Hayward Company)
Attleboro, MA

Founded in 1851 as Thompson, Hayward & Company in Mechanicsville, CT. In 1855 Charles Hayward and Jonathan Briggs became partners. When they parted ways Walter Hayward joined his father and the company became known as CE Hayward Co. In 1887 George Sweet became a partner and the name changed to Hayward & Sweet Co. Around 1904 the company name changed to Walter E. Hayward Co and in 1908 the company changed hands but the name remained the same, until 1971 when it was merged with another company under the same ownership to form Amtel Arts, Inc.

Alvin H. Hankins

Room 5-8 Madison Block
Seattle, WA
Last know address - no longer in business
1425 4th Ave Ste 901
Seattle, WA 98101-2222

(206) 623-5861

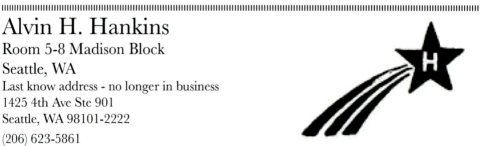

It is known the company was in existence as early as 1913 and still in business in the 1920's. One of the employees of the company was Mr. Godfrey Emanuel Lundberg, who engraved the Lord's Prayer on the tiny head of a gold pin that was displayed at the 1915 Panama-Pacific Exposition in San Francisco and won a gold medal in engraving. It is not known what insignia or medals may have been made by this company.

Harding (Newell Harding & Co.?)
Boston, MA. I

Their is a bit on confusion and hopefully this clears some of it up. New Harding is mentioned but it is incorrect.

Newell Harding was formed in 1822, they introduced the use of power to roll silver. The company was sold in 1832 to Ward & Rich. But the name continued to be used into the 1860's. They made flatware and silver objects such as tea pots.

The second listing is for Harding Uniform and Regalia Co. that is believed to have been formed in 1900. The firm appears to have recently gone out of business.

Last known address
Harding Uniform & Regalia Co
35rescent Ave, Braintree, MA 02184
781-848-0740

Hartegen
Newark, NH.
No information on this supplier.

Hartmann Inc.   IOH H23
No information on this supplier.

Havens & Co
New York, NY
Manufacturer of class rings, pins and medals.

103

A.J. Hawkins I
No information on this supplier.

H.E. Heacock Co.
Manila, Philippines I
This was a retail store founded in 1900 by Mr. H E Heacock selling men's watches, chains and cuff links but clocks, silverware, cut glass and other general merchandise. In 1909 H.E. Heacock and his partner, Freer, sold the business to Samuel Gaches and other partners. The store continued to grow and became larger moving from one building to another and to an 8 story building that was brought down by an earthquake caused the destruction of the building on the Escolta, shutting down business. But within 30 days they were back in business. Much of the building was destroyed during the Battle of Manila however the business did survive and was brought back to life during the reconstruction period of 1946-1948. It was still a viable and popular department store in the Fifties. They had a jewelry department complete with manufacturing capability.

B. Hecker
New York and Indianapolis. I
It is believed they were a metal stamping company based on the products shown below. No insignia have been found with their hallmark.

Heckethorn Mfg. & Supply Co.
215 Main Street (where it was founded)
Littleton, CO.
Current:
Heckethorn Manufacturing
2005 Forrest Street
Dyersburg, TN 38024

Founded in 1938, it was incorporated in 1939 by William R. Heckethorn. They started by making pullys and hardware. When WWII started they converted to manufacturing photographic products and hardware specialties such as 20mm projectiles and 4.2 inch chemical mortar fuses. When the war was over, Heckethorn successfully converted his company to peacetime uses, manufacturing specialty hardware, photographic products and war medals. In 1957 Heckethorn closed the Littleton plant. Thus ending military production. Nickname for the company was HECO.

The Hefter-Reib Co.
43-51, West 4th Street
New York, NY

It is believed the company came into being at the start of WWI (1913) and was dissolved in 1917. They did not sell direct to the military or personnel but to other manufacturers.

Jack Heller ("H" in a circle) IOH H21

Believed to have only made Paratrooper Badges during WWII, two different locations of the same hallmark have been found. The company was later issued IOH number H21 but it appears it was never used.

Wilhelm Helding
Leipzig, Germany I
No information on this supplier.

The Henderson-Ames Co.
Kalamazoo, MI. I

Frank Henderson first moved to Kalamazoo from Dowagiac in 1860 and formed a saddlery business with Charles Brown in 1866. After buying out his partner a few years later, Henderson expanded his business in 1868 by adding uniforms and regalia. Henderson formed a new partnership in 1870 with T. F. Giddings, but the two partners split three years later; Henderson maintained the new regalia division while Giddings kept the saddlery division. In 1893, the Henderson-Ames Company was officially formed when Henderson consolidated with the Chicago branch of the Ames Sword Company in Chicopee, Massachusetts. In 1933, the Henderson-Ames Company merged with another regalia firm, the Lilley Company of Columbus, Ohio, to form the Lilley-Ames Company. Operations were soon moved to Ohio, effectively ending the company's affiliation with Kalamazoo and their name. Known for uniforms and swords.

Herdon Recognition

IOH H34

7800 SW Barbur Blvd
Portland, OR 97219
(503) 244-1165

Began business to provide graduation nurse pins and associated graduation products to hospital programs for nursing education and universities buying from other suppliers. Then started it own production. Today they are a full scale recognition company.

Eli Hertzberg Jewelry Company

San Antonio, TX

During WWI the jewelry store was located across the street from Frank Brothers who made uniforms. Items hallmarked form the Frank Brothers may have been made by Hertzberg.

Hickok Manufacturing Co.

USMC QM 170

299 State St
Rochester, NY

Hickok Manufacturing Company founded in 1909 by S. Rae Hickok, when he purchased a small jewelry plating business for $350.

When he died in 1945, Mr. Raymond P. Hickok inherited the company presidency at the age of 27. Three years later he added the title of chairman. He led the company's expansion as a major manufacturer of wallets, belts, pants, suspenders, cuff links, tie clasps and other men's accessories. In 1988 it became part of the Tandy Corp.

February 10, 1948
US Trademark
71549248.

Hess & Albertson
St. Louis, MO. I
No known information.

Michael Hessberg, Inc.   IOH   H32N
180 Autumn Street
Passaic, NJ 07055
973-777-8700
See listing for Bende & Sons Inc. Same company.

Hilborn & Hamburger, Inc.   (H&H) IOH H-24, H-24-N
122 Dayton Ave
Passaic, NJ 07055
USMC Quartermaster ID 135, 307, 362, 368, 397, 622
HILBORN-HAMBURGER, INC. was formed on June 29, 1926 in New York by Jerome M. Hilborn & Jerome M. Hamburger they had been working for N.S. Meyer.
H&H Purchased Imperial around 1942.
They did not register their trademark until 1961 and the company went out of business in 2007 or 2008 after Hilborn-Hamburger Inc. was accused of substituting various cheaper plated metal for brass, and other less-expensive materials as part of more than $12 million worth of insignia items sold to the military since 1999. In a settlement reached, the company agreed to pay a fine of $251,000 to settle federal charges. They never recovered from this fine and went out of business.

High Flight HOA H26
3362 Mather Field Road
Rancho, CA 95670
No information on this business.

Carl Hirsch & Sons Iron and Rail Co.
St. Louis, MO. I
Founded in September 1905. No additional information.

M. Fred Hirsch Co.
Jersey City, NJ c. 1920-1945
A flat wear company but may have made these during WWII.

G. Hirsch & Sons IOH H31N
1040 Ave. of Americas
New York NY 10018
Founded January 1965 and dissolved June 1985.

HLI Lordship Industries, Inc. IOH H25, L1, L22
Hauppauge, NY.
See Lordship Industries for details.

W. H. Horstmann & Sons
Philadelphia, PA. I
Founded, in 1815, by William H. Horstmann and was in business until 1947 mainly of silk weaving. Sold buttons, swords, etc Started out selling lace and woven military goods. In the 1850's they imported swords, they subcontracted much of the insignia and items they sold.

Huguenin Freres & Co
le Locle, Switzerland

Founded in 1868 two young craftsmen, Fritz Huguenin, and his brother Albert. They became well known for watch cases. They also made stamping of medals and insignia. During WWII they made some US wings, In 1999 the company merged with Paul Kramer and in 2002 Huguenin + Kramer joined with Faude, giving birth to the current company Faude & Huguenin SA, headcurtered in Gippingen

Humrichous Co
Memphis, TN. (HR). W

Sometimes you see this spelled as Homrichous which is not correct. Several of these wings have appeared in pictures of men in uniform. No information can be found on this concern. However most of these wings are not hallmarked. The hallmark shows the correct spelling.

Hullin
Atlanta, GA

No information is known about this company. The badge appears to be early WWII based on the fittings on the back.

Imperial Insignia Manufacturing Company
(later Hilborn-Hamberger/Imperial)

Purchased by Hilborn-Hamberger in 1942.

Insignia Co of America
No information has been found on this concern.

Inter-All Corp.   IOH I24
31 Wesr State St
Granby, MA 01033
(413) 467-7181

Contract embroidery on clothing and accessory items as well as the manufacture of both embroidered appliqués and emblems.

International Enterprises Ltd   IOH T21
230 Oak St
Providence, RI 02909
201-866-5893

International Insignia Corp   IOH II-C, I-21
1280 Eddy Street
Providence, RI
02905-4534
401.784.0000
www.internationalinsignia.com

International Insignia Corporation was founded in 1954 specializing in the manufacture of Military Insignia. International Insignia works closely with Vanguard Industries for all its custom work. They currently work in brass and are a major supplier to Vanguard. They also manufactured for Meyer and H&H in the past.

Interstate Lace Co.   IOH I23
717 10th St
Union City, NJ 07087
(201) 866-5592
Is a Mfg Schiffli Embroideries Pleating/stitching Services company.

Ira Greene Co.   IOH 3G, G3, G23
New York, NY/Providence, RI.
http://www.iragreen.com

Ira Geene, Inc. was founded in 1943 in Providence, Rhode Island. They are one of the few remaining manufacturers of US insignia still in business. Sta-BriteTM is one of their mainstay items. They still manufacture all Paratrooper Badges and the Air Assault Badge in sterling silver. Ira Green Corp purchased the following companies, Krew, Inc in October 2002 and HLI Lordship Industries, Inc in October 1999.

Iron & Russell

95 Chestnut St
Providence, RI

Charles F. Irons established the business in 1861 making jewelry. Mr. Charles Russell started work as an errand boy in 1875 and worked his way up by hard work and continuing his education. In 1881 he became a partner and in 1893 the company name was changed to Iron & Russell. In 1968 the company was sold to S. Scarf, Inc. and is a division of Barrows Industries.

Irvine & Jachens

San Francisco, CA
6700 Mission Street
Daly City, Calif. 94014
650-755-4715
www.irvineandjachensbadges.com

The business was founded in 1886 at Kearny and Market Streets in San Franciso. In 1906 the great earthquake and fire destroyed the growing business, and the firm started over again in the 2100 block on Market Street. Later the business moved to 1027 Market Street. In 1926, the business again moved, this time to 1068 Mission Street, which was near 7th Street, next to the Main Post Office. The firm was now called Irvine & Jachens, and in the 24 years that followed, became a land-mark in San Francisco.

A change of landlord and growing pains made a new location imperative. As the firm also owned a brand-new factory making silver goods just south of San Francisco, Irvine & Jachens, Inc. moved again and is now housed all under one roof at 6700 Mission Street in Daly City, California.

During WWII they did make some insignia and these are very rare. The current production centers around police and fire badges and belt buckles.

Jacqueline Embroidery Co.
2119 Whitesville RD
Toms River, NJ. (J23) (textile)
(732) 363-3240
http://www.jacqueline.com
Founded in 1978, little is know about this company. Narrow Fabric Mills and Schiffli Machine Embroidery.

Jaurez
See The Walter Lampel Co. (script "WL" in a shield)
New York, NY.
"Jaurez Wings" was a nickname given to a specific designed wings that were believed to have been made in Mexico during WWII but were made in the Walter Lampl factory in Newark, NJ. Very rare to find one with the Lampel hallmark.

Warren Jay Products Corp.
New York, NY. (1J) I
No information concerning this firm.

Jaymac Bowling Supplies   IOH J22
PO Box 10331
Erie, PA 16514
(814) 825-3263
Established in 1982 to sell bowling apparel and accessories. They also sell trophies and medals.

Jenkel Jewelers
San Diego, CA
Made wings for Army Air Corp and Navy in very small quantities during WWII.

116

Jessop Jeweler
401 West C Street
San Diego, CA 92101
(619) 234 - 4137
www.jessopjeweler.com

Founded by Joseph Jessop in 1892. A watchmaker from Lythem, England his forst store was at 952 Fifth Avenue in downtown San Diego. He continued to run the company for the next 40 years. Then his family continued to run the business until 1970 when it was sold to Dayton Hudson Corporation, which today is known as Target Corporation. But in 1973 George Carter Jessop started up the business again under his name. In 1997 the company bought back the original name and became Jessop's again under the fifth generation of the family.

Jostens, Inc.
Princeton, IL/Owatonna & Minneapolis, MN. I, W

In 1897 by Otto Josten, opened a small jewelry and watch repair business located in Owatonna, Minnesota. In 1900 the founder began manufacturing emblems and awards for nearby schools and in 1906, the year of incorporation, Josten added class rings to his product line, to be sold to schools throughout the Midwest. By 1930 the company sold only class rings. During WWII the company adapting its plant and equipment to manufacture precision parts and insignia. After the war they returned to class rings and expanded into yearbooks. They are still a major ring manufacturer.

JMS Jewelry Co in business between 1940-and 1960 in Bloomfield, NJ.
or
JMS
Shanholtz Joseph M Jeweler
118 S 8th St
Philadelphia, PA 19107
(215) 627-0911
or
J.M. Schriade
Chicago, IL. I
These hallmarks have been "guessed" as belonging to these three concerns in various books or Internet cites.

Arthur Johnson Manufacturing Co
14 Church St
New York, NY

Johnson 1836 srl
Via Milano, 252
20021 Baranzate (MI)
Italia

Established in 1836 by James Johnson from Birmingham, England, at the in Borghetto di Porta Orientale in Milano as a manufacturer producing buttons and metal ornaments, continuing his work originally held in Birmingham and later in Lyon. In 1847 the business passed to Stefano Johnson, who styled the business, Stabilimento Stefano Johnson, and the emphasis moved to the manufacture of medals and military and livery insignia. In 1880 Federico Johnson, was the prominent figure in the business in the firm and started production of Art Medals using the skills of the sculptors Pogliaghi, Bistolfi, Calandra, Boninsegna, the company was able to make a significant contribution especially in the Art Nouveau style, producing medals of great artistic quality.

The company managed to survive the difficult period between the two world wars, but in 1943 their workshops at Corso di Porta Nuova were heavily bombed.

The post-war economic recovery allowed Caesar Johnson, who was now heading the company, to relaunch their manufacturing activity in the new settlement of Baranzate, just outside Milano, the current headquarters of the company. Their Rome branch in the 1960's was the site of numerous exhibitions of contemporary medalists.

In 2003 the company restyled its name to 1836 JOHNSON, reminiscent of the official founding year.

Registrations
May 27, 1935
March 26, 1968
May 29, 2003

Johnson National
New York.

IOH J21

Joy Insignia Inc
219 Goolsby Blvd.
Deerfield Beach, FL 33441
(954) 426-9100
Embroidery company established in 1970.

Kaag Manufacturers, Inc.
Los Angeles, CA
Believed to have been in business in the 1960's as a trophy company and also was found to make some badges.

Hallmark from Los Angeles police badge.

Martin Kahn

IOH 6k

Bronx, NY.
Manufactured DIs in the late 1950's.

Kalka Maschinenstickerei GbR
Bgm.-Bohl-Strasse 21
86157 Augsburg
Germany
Founded in the 1950's as a manufacturer of embroidery products and still in business.

Katzson Brothers
960 Vallejo St.
Denver, CO 80204
303-893-3535
http://www.katzson.com

Founded approximately in 1940. This company is a wholesale distributor and did not manufacture any insignia. It is believed they sold to Base Exchanges and to Army-Navy Surplus type stores. Their insignia was only hallmarked by metal content and did not have any company names. Still in business but only provides hotel supplies, Laundry and Dry Cleaning Supplies.

K. B. Specialties   IOH K25
Bellflower, CA (KBS). I
Manufactured DI's.

Kel-lac Uniforms Inc.   IOH K27
7016 Highway 90 West
San Antinto, TX 78227
(210) 674-0511
A uniform and tactical hardware supplier. Authorized AF Advantage program and GSA.

Kennedy Inc   IOH K28
21 CIRCUIT DRIVE
NORTH KINGSTOWN, RI 02852
401-295-7800
www.kennedy-inc.com

Founded approximately 40 years ago. Authorized to manufacture medals.

Wilbur C. Kiff Co.
Attleboro, MA
Manufacturer of medals and insignia.

IOH K22

P. J. King
Melbourne, Australia
Located in Victoria in 1937

The Kinney Co.
Providence, RI ("K Co." in a shield) W
Founded around 1907. In business at least into the 1970's.

IOH K24

Harry Klitzner Co., Inc.
Providence, RI
Founded in 1907 by 14 year old Harry Klitzer and still in business today as a manufacturer of fraternal emblematic jewelry.

Klammer
Innsbruck, Austria. I
No information on this firm.

Karl J. Klein
511 SW Washington St
Portland, OR 97204
Phone: (503) 226-6748
It was established in 1926 and currently operates as Klein Jewelers.

Konwal (Western Military Supply)
Japan. I
See listing under Western Military Supply.

Krew, Inc.   IOH 1K, K21 (Not Assigned hallmark KI)
Attleboro, MA.
Was founded in 1950 by Raymond U. Kelliher who served in the U.S. Army in WWII. It apparently was a family owned business until 1978. In October 2002 Ira Green Inc. purchased the company assets.

Kyoto
Kyoto Prefecture, Japan

Kyoto s a city in the central part of the island of Honsh, Japan. It formerly was the imperial capital of Japan, it is now the capital of Kyoto Prefecture, as well as a major part of the Kyoto-Osaka-Kobe metropolitan area. It is very possible that a jeweler or insignia manufacturer made Paratrooper badges and in the same way that Sendai badges were marked with the name of the city of manufacture. During WWII the city was largely spared from conventional bombing, although small-scale air raids did result in casualties. So industry may have been available to produce such items since the area was known for artisans in small plants.

Some US Army units were stationed in this area after the war.

Laorer
Los Angeles, CA. I
No information on this company.

Walter Lampl Co
New York, Newark, NJ, Juarez, Mexico

Founded by Walter Lampl in 1921 he died in 1921 and the business was continued by his wife and sons until they closed the operations down in 1959. During WWII they made a series of wings which became called "Juarez Wings" a nickname given to these specific designed wings that were believed to have been made in Mexico during WWII but were made in the Walter Lampl factory in Newark, NJ. They had jewelry made in Mexico which added to this nickmane. Very rare to find one with the Lampl hallmark. Many just had block lettering of either STERLING or COIN SILVER.

G is upside down.

L. Christian Lauer

Nurnberg, Germany. I

Sulzbacher Straße 47, 90552 Röthenbach an der Pegnitz, Germany

Lauer is a family business founded in 1729 by Johann Jabob Lauer, but in 1848 it became well known under the leadership of Ludwig Christoph Lauer. They were best known for minting Jetons and toy coins. Later they became prolific producers of wertmarken, mostly generic tokens to be used by businesses. During WWII they were located in Nürnberg Germany manufacturing Medals, Badges, and Insignia for the German Military. During WWII they employed forced laborers. During the occupation period, they did the same but for the US Army. Today, the company is still in business under the name of L. Chr. Lauer GmbH with 90% of their current production for the automobile industry. They no longer manufacturer insignia.

In 1941 it was decided to create the Administration of German Orders Manufacturers (deutschen Ordenhersteller), known as the LDO. 14 is the number assigned to this company. They were also assigned Nazi manufacturer ID RMZ 13

Leary's Military Company   IOH L28

155 Frederick St

Newark, DE 19702

302-838-0102

Established in 2002 in 2010 a new business was started by the same owner called Learys Military Co. located at 2304 Porter Rd, Bear, De 19701 the IOH number was assigned to the new company.

Leavens Manufacturing Co. (Leavens Awards)
Summer St.
Attleboro, MA. (L21) I

Founded on March 18,1948 by Theodore Leavens, Lucy Fantaccione, Pete Taratian, Rauul LaCasse, as Armstrong & Haig Abdian. Acquired by Oneida Ltd. in the mid-1970's and changed hands in 1985 purchased by the Fleet Family. The company closed on August 31, 1999.

Leonard Embroidery Company   IOH 2L, L23
323-331 E. Allegheny Ave
Philadelphia PA 19134   215-426-6646

It is believe the company was in business in WWII based on a newspaper article on patches in 1945.
They had a trademark filed on 8/19/1959 of SWISS-TEX
They also had listed a metal products division. It was renewed in 1982 and was canceled in 2002 for failure to renew.

LEONARD
PHILA
2L

Letters Medals Inc.   IOH   L29
Road 176 KM 5.8 Camino Los Andinos
San Juan, PR 00928
301-363-1000
CAGE 0JXD9

The trademark was filed for in 1985 and canceled in 1992. This trademark was for jewelry. No other information has been found.

Trademark
#73516123
Jan. 03, 1985

LeVelle & Co.
Philadelphia, PA/Washington, D.C. I, W

They are known to have made DI's and two types of wings -- Pilot and Aircrew during WWII.

Liberty Emblem Co.

Made sweetheart items during WWII, not much known about this company. Not to be confused with a current company with the same name that was started in 1989 selling police and fire badges.

R. Liebmann Manufacturing Company
Newark, N.J
WWI Button - no other record.

H. F. Linder Co.
1441 Third Ave
New York, NY

Founded July 1915 by Herman F. Linder and Herman Malz. In July 1916 Mr. Malz sold his interest to Sohpie Westphal. The business filed for bankruptcy in May 1917. The business sold pro-German jewelry.

The M. C. Lilly Co.
Columbus, OH

Established in the mid 1860's by Mitchell Campbell Lilley, John Siebert and the brothers, Charles and Henry Lindenberg. Following the depression in 1933, the company was acquired by Henderson-Ames of Kalamazoo, Michigan and the name was changed to Lilley-Ames. The company are thought to have gone out of business in 1965.

William Link & Co.
("WL Co" in 2 linked ovals) W
407 Mulberry St
Newark, NJ

Established in 1871 by William Link, in 1882 they became Link & Conkluing and went back to their original name in 1886. A few years later in 1893 the name changed to Link, Ahgell & Weiss and in 1900 they changed again to Link & Angell and this listed until 1910 when they became William Link & Co and as can be seem in the advertisement below claimed to be "Largest producers of Officers insignia in the world." Prior to WWI they did not manufacture military insignia. During WWI they moved almost all their production to the war effort. In 1924 they became Link & Angell again and vanish by 1930.

Linz Brothers Jewelers
Dallas, TX. W

Linz Brothers, a jewelry firm, grew from the efforts of five brothers. Joseph and Elias Linz of St. Louis opened the firm of Joseph Linz and Brother in Denison in October 1877. In 1882 Ben Linz joined the firm. When Elias died in 1883, his interest in the partnership was taken by Simon. In 1884 Albert Linz joined the firm and in 1890 became a partner. Ben became a partner in 1897. In 1891 the firm moved to Dallas. Joseph Linz retired in 1907, and the firm's name was changed to Linz Brothers. It appears they are no longer in business. It is believed they only made a few items during WWI.

Lord and Taylor

Lord & Taylor is headquartered in New York City, and is the oldest luxury department store in North America. As a retail operation these would have been made by another concern, just for them to sell.

HLI Lordship Industries, Inc.   IOH L1, L22
Hauppauge, NY.

In 1996 Lordship Industries was fined $80,000 for selling 300 bootleg Medals of Honor. H.L.I. Lordship Industries Inc. of Hauppage, N.Y., also will give the government $22,500 it received for illegally selling the bogus medals for $75 apiece at memorabilia shows from 1991 to 1994. Lordship had been one of the largest manufacturers of US Medals and the only Medal of Honor manufacturer prior pleading guilty of these charges. The owner of the company made 300 extra MOHs and sold them to a friend who went to military shows and sold them off to anyone. The company lost all its contracts and in April 1999 it was purchased by Ira Green Corp and by October 1999 had ceased all operations.

Note: Authorized L1(number 1) they sometimes marked item LI (letter I) for Lordship Industries. They also did not change hallmarks from product to product such as pre and post 1965. They were not very good at being consistent with their hallmarking.

Note the hallmark is HLP - "His Lordship Products"

Hallmark on top of the flat back silver plated brass appears to be Korean War era.

Los Angeles Rubber Stamp Co.
Los Angeles, CA (LARS). I

It is not known when this company started or ended, but references date as early as 1890 and as late as 1933.

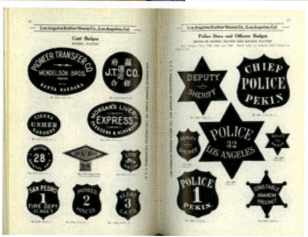

1920's catalog

131

Louisville Mfg. Co.

IOH   L25

No information on this company.

Ludlow & Co.
London, England

Company's name was originally Barnet Ludski & Son, a maker of surgical instruments founded in 1867. In 1884 the name changed to Ludski B & Son. In 1933 the name changed to Ludlow & Co, due to the family changing their last name and it is believe due to antisemitism. In 1941 did they incorporate. It is believed that around 1891 they switched from surgical instruments to military insignia. Also the hallmarks would have been Ludski & Son, London prior to 1933 and Ludlow London after. It is not known if or when they ceased operations.

K. G. Luke Co.
Melbourne, Australia

In the 1920's Kenneth George Luke started his metal craft business in Melbourne Australia. By the start of WWII it had grown into a company of 650 employees. They appeared to have vanished in 1976.

W. Lutz
Furth, Germany. I

No information on this concern.

Luxenberg
485 Madison Ave
New York, NY

Morrie Luxenberg was a tailor in New York City and also famous for having the best looking insignia made. The insignia was mostly made by Blackinton for Luxenberg, but they did not use the dies for any other maker. Today these are among the most sought after WWII wings and badges. Some wings were also made by AECO company called the third pattern. Luxenberg hat badges and buttons were also made by J R Gaunt of Birmingham, England. In 2007 Weingarten Gallery obtained the rights to the Luxenberg Trademark.

1st Pattern 2nd Pattern 3rd Pattern
              Blackinton   AE Co.

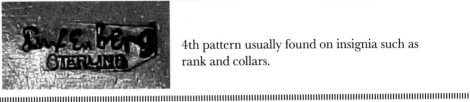

4th pattern usually found on insignia such as rank and collars.

Maco-Boch
New York, NY
WWII manufacturer of sweetheart pins.

Magic Novelty Co. Inc.   IOH M30
308 Dyckman St
New York, NY 10034
(212) 304-2777
Founded by Herman Neuburger about 65 years ago in upper Manhattan. They are a major supplier of stamped products and findings. Still in business.

Marlow White Co.
400 Seneca St
Leavenworth, KS 66048
The company was founded by John Biskupovic who opened a small uniform shop in 1879. He was an immigrant who came to Florida and worked in shipyards at first, because of his complex name the other workers called him "Whitey" he later adopted the last name White. At the end of WWII Marlow took over the Army element of the business and in 1971 they opened a store with the Post Exchange at Ft. Leavenworth. In 1990 the company was invited by the Army and Air Force Exchange System to become its premier line of dress uniforms offered in Exchanges throughout the world. The company continues to grow and now provides Navy uniforms as well as police and fire uniforms. They do not manufacture insignia or medals.

Marples and Beasley

The company was registered in June 1902 in the Chester, UK Assay Office as a business in Birmingham. They were bought out in 1936 by Rebus, but they continued to use the original name. They were a significant and bone fide supplier to the War Office and produced both KC & QC era badges and buttons. They supplied large volumes during WWII. The company was run until 1991 when the factory in Birmingham was closed down. However in British collecting circles they are known for re-strikes.

S. Mars, Inc
New York, NY

IOH M31N

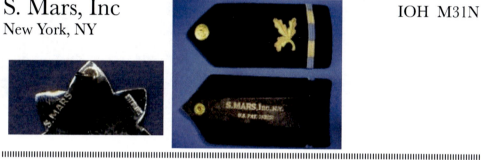

Marshall Field & Company
AKA Marshall Field's

Was an upscale department store in Chicago, Il that was founded in 1852 by Potter Palmer that grew to become a major chain before being acquired by Macy's, Inc. on August 30, 2005. They had a silver department and made sterling products. It is not certain they made this wing but the hallmark matches.

Jerry Massey W
No information on this listing.

Joseph Mayer M
Seattle, WA

Manufacturer founded in 1897 by Joseph Mayer and his brothers, Albert and Markus. They became the largest manufacturing jewelers on the West Coast with as many as 150 people working in their factory becoming the largest manufacturing jewelers on the west coast. Albert and Markus split off from Joseph in 1920, the business continued as Joseph Mayer Inc. and then as Joseph Mayer Co. In 1937 Joseph passed and shortly after so did his company being acquired by the E.J. Towle Mfg. Co. in 1938;

Joseph Mayr
Linz, Austria. I

No information on this listing.

McCabe Brothers   IOH M23
New York, NY. I
45 John St
New York, NY 10038
212-227-9418

Medals of America

114 Southchase Boulevard
Fountain Inn, SC 29644
www.medalsofamerica.com
800-308-0849

The company was founded in 1976 By Frank and Linda Foster while he was on active duty with the US Army, upon retirement in 1990 they moved the company to South Carolina and later to their current address.

US Trademark 77814218

Medallic Art Co.

New York, NY. I, M

Founded by Henry Weil, "a highly respected French sculptor living in New York City." in 1903. The company moved to Danbury, Connecticut in 1972, Sioux Falls, South Dakota in 1991 then to Dayton, Nevada in 1997 where it currently operates. In July 2009, Medallic Art Company was purchased by Northwest Territorial Mint.

The Metalcraft Mint Inc.   IOH M33
2660 West Mason St
Green Bay, WI 54303
920-593-1531 800-558-6348
Sage 52575
Founded in 1948 is a die striking company and is currently an active supplier to the US.

Merit Ribbon Co.   IOH M26
30 Davids Dr
Hauppauge NY 11788-2005
516-231-9779
Cage Code 4A218
Founded in 1982 and ceased to exist in 1982. No other information.

Mermod, Jaccard & King
St. Louis, MO. I
Founded by D.C. Jaccard and A.S. Mermod as Mermod & Jaccard, in 1864 becoming Mermod, Jaccard & Co. in 1873. Goodman King joined the firm in 1865 and the name was changed to Mermod, Jaccard & King Jewelry Co. in 1905. Primarily retailers and jewelers, also made some sterling and silver-plate flatware, hollowware and souvenir spoons, but was outsourcing all of its silver manufacturing by 1890. They creased operations in the 1980's.

Metal Arts Co.   IOH M30
800 St Paul
Rochester, NY. (AMACO)
The Rochester firm was founded in 1913. It struck medals over the years and created a division called American Mint for striking coin-relief medals about 1970. Metal Arts no longer manufactures medals but apparently is in the metal parts cleaning service business for industrial clients.

G.C.Meyer Company
Indianapolis, IN. I
No information on this company.

N.S. Meyer
New York, NY.
1868- 2000s

IOH 9M, M22

Meyer was founded in 1868 by Nathan S. Meyer and is a very interesting company since they were a sales agency and not a true manufacturer. They never made anything but rather contracted the manufacturer to many companies and then acted as a sales agent to the government and anyone else who wanted to buy. For example in 1911 they held a contract to supply buttons made by Gaunt & Sons. Thus it becomes very hard to date many of their items since they did not care too much. Their primary existence was just based on moving product. Because of this their is a wide variety of items with their hallmark.

In 1999 they were charged by the US Government for price fixing and it force them out of business. Vanguard Industries purchased their remaining inventory, good will and rights to their name on July 17, 2000.

A major problem with Meyer is that many of their dies were sold off after they closed their doors and re-strikes have been made using the original dies.

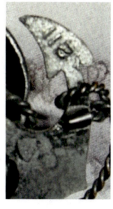

Trademarked March 06, 1924. Currently owned by VANGUARD INDUSTRIES EAST, INC., Norfolk, VA 23502. TM serial number of 71193344.

 Trademarked March 06, 1924, 71193345, expired 1/10/1986

In the 20's : screwback, "N.S. MEYER, INC. NEW YORK" (raised), no shield
Early 30's : screwback, "N.S. MEYER NEW YORK" + shield (engraved).
Mid 30's to 1943 : screwback, "N.S. MEYER, INC. NEW YORK" + shield (engraved).
WWII : pinback, "N.S. MEYER, INC. NEW YORK" + shield (raised)
Late 40's : Shield only (raised)
Late 40's to early 50's : "N.S. MEYER, INC. NEW YORK" + shield (raised and 1/2 size)
Early 50's : "N.S. MEYER, INC. N.Y.C" or "N.S. MEYER, INC. N.Y.©" + shield (raised)
Mid 50's to Mid 60's : "N.S. MEYER, INC NY" or "N.S. MEYER, INC NEW YORK" + Shield + 9M (raised).
Mid 60's to mid 70's : N.S. MEYER, INC. NEW YORK" + shield + 22M (raised)
Since mid 70's : N.S. MEYER, INC. NEW YORK MADE IN USA" + shield + 22M (raised).
Source : Militaria magazine, issue 272, mars 2008, p. 43.

The following is from an article by Bob Capistrano

These illustrations are from an article I wrote for the Trading Post back in 1986 as a first stab at trying to date hallmarks. Needless to say, they are somewhat out of date, but they and the article did hit a chord. In the early 1990s, prodded by Paul O'Dowd, a number of DI collectors systematically surveyed our collections to see how educated our guesses actually were. When it came to Meyer, we turned up close to 50 variations, mostly minor variants of the basic types illustrated in the article. The most glaring error in my article was in dating raised hallmarks with "N.Y.C." under the name and above the shield. The late '40s early '50s original estimate was based on the mark being found on some postwar pieces, e.g., the MP School. However, it turned up on a number of WW2 pieces such as the 893rd TD Bn, HD of Chesapeake Bay, some AAF pieces whose names escape me, etc. One of these days I'll update my article, but then again I've said that for 15 years ...

The most important thing to keep in mind was that Meyer (and Dondero) were jobbers who subcontracted DI manufacturing to other small firms. This explains why so many hallmarks existed contemporaneously. WW2, for example, saw the "N.S. Meyer, Inc. / New York" above the shield in both incised and raised; the name and place alongside the shield (in two lines); the name and place in three lines beside the shield; and the "NYC" variant. Several of these added "sterling" when the manufacture of brass DI was forbidding in late 1942.

Among the changes/additions to the 1986 chart I would make today are:

1. The earliest Meyer hallmark may be a two line "N.S.MEYER,INC / NEW-YORK" in an art nouveau font without a shield (found on the 1st CA and 6th Composite Gp DIs, indicating a jobber who got the contract for early DIs worn in Panama)
2. Another early one is "Meyer Metal" in two lines with an arrow between the words. This one is also seen in a lot of brass from the 1920s and 1930s.
3. One for c. 1940-42 is a three line raised hallmark "N.S. Meyer / Inc / New York" found on a number of DIs including the 501st Pcht Inf Bn (Thunderbird) worn only in 1940-41, dumped for the plastic Indian head when the Bn was expanded into a regt, the original design not reappearing until the mid 1950s when the 501st (inactive since 1946) was reactivated.

J. A. Meyers & Co.
620 Metropolitan Bldg
Los Angeles, CA   I

Founded in 1912 and was sold by the original family in 1977 to Halcom Industries and continues to operate as a subsidiary manufacturing recognition jewelry.

Theo Meyer Badgemaker
9 Nixon St
Gret Lynn, Auckland
New Zealand

Founded in 1921 by Theodore Meyer. During WWII Vice Admiral Halsey had them supply the US Navy with insignia.

Midwest Trophy Co.   IOH M29
Del City, OK. I
Currently -- MTM Recognition
3201 SE 29th
Oklahoma City, OK 73115
(877) 686.7464
www.mtmrecognition.com

Midwest Trophy Manufacturing began in David R. Smith's garage in Del City in 1971. It is now known as MTM Recognition,

Mil-Bar Plastic Inc   IOH M39
441 Leroy Drive
Corona, CA 92879
951-272-4822
http://www.mil-bar.com
Founded approximately 45 years ago and are known for the plastic ribbon bar holders which they patented in 1958. Also manufactured ribbons.

Military Art & Emblem Co.
Hyattsville, MD. I
No information on this supplier.

Military Equipment Corp.   IOH M32N
89 Hqs. North Tower, 14th Floor
Morristown, NJ 07960
No information on this supplier.

Military Manufacturer's of Maryland   IOH G18, M24
(by Gordons Fort Meade).
Gordon's
No information on this supplier.

Military Post Suppliers   IOH 7M, M7, M21
771 McCarter Pwky
Newark, NJ. 07102 Sales office also in Japan

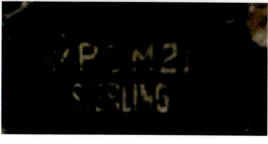

 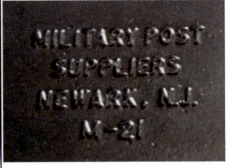

See note on bottom of card

Military Service Co.
3500 Blue Lake Drive
Suite 150
Birmingham, AL 35243

800-255-3722

http://militaryservicecompany.com/

Military Service Company in 1994 became part of and was the oldest division of EBSCO Industries Inc, organically founded in 1941 during World War II and provides an array of goods and services that serve the U.S. military. The Birmingham, AL-based company's popular military commemoratives inventory includes challenge coins for the Army, Navy, Air Force, Marines, Coast Guard, Veterans, National Guard as well as military-themed license plate holders, pens and more.

No known insignia or medals made by the company. In July 2009, Military Service Company's challenge coin business was purchased by Northwest Territorial Mint. Now it is part of EBSCO Industries. Some of its items may have been manufactured by Vulcan Industries (V-22).

Logo, no hallmark

J. Milton
New York. I
No information on this business.

Minero-Newcome Co IOH 1M, M28
New York NY. I
Made DIs during WWII and later. Believed to have been started in the 1920's. Cited in a number of books and catalogs of awards for Archery. The company was incorporated in 1970 and ceased to exist in 1981.

Minister
Columbus, OH. I
No information on this business.

Monarch Military Products Co., Inc.   IOH M12
New York, NY. I

Moody Bros.
Los Angeles, CA. W

Brothers Joseph A Moody and Frank S Moody.
Based on Patents they were in a Partnership with Leo R. Panwels in a company called Paramount Watchband Manufacturing Company in Los Angles in the late 1930's.

Morgan's
San Francisco, CA. I

No information on this company.

Motex Inc.   IOH   M36
6210 Monroe Pl
West New York, NY 07093
864-862-6051

Founded in 1995 as a badge manufacturer no additional information is known.

Mourgeon
4 Royal Park
Paris France. I

Many badges from pre-WWII have been found. Since they were listed by the IOH they must have made some US insignia after the war. Also found several modern French insignia.

Loren Murchison & Co.   IOH   M27
Attleboro, MA. I

The company was founded by Loren Murchison who was an Olympic sprinters in the 1920 and 1924 games. In 1925 Murchison developed spinal meningitis and was paralyzed for the rest of his life from the waist down. He ran a company manufacturing sports medals and jewelry. They were known for ceramic and metal mugs with a metal logo on them. The last known record of the company was a filling for a trade-mark in 1981.

Nanco

It is believed this NANCO was in business from the 1920's to the late 1930's. Due to the name not much can be found as many business used the same name and still do. The primary focus was Naval insignia.

National Badge & Insignia Co.
Japan/Washington, DC. (NBI Japan) I

No information on this company.

National Decoration Co.
Shanghai, China (NDC). I

No information on this company.

National Die & Button Mold   IOH   N28
462 Barell Ave.
Carlstadt, NJ 07072
201-939-1870

Founded in 1911 engages in manufacturing metal stampings, novelty trim, and functional hardware and uniform/military badges.

National Guard Equipment Company
155 East 34st
New York. (NGBC). I

Pre-War catalog. Insignia in the catalog are stock items.

N.B.I.
Japan. I

Post WWII and believed to have made insignia until after the Korean War.

Nellie's Alteration & Mfg.   IOH   N29
5415 Beacon Pkwy E
Birmingham, AL 35223
(205) 870-5283

They have been in business for about 30 years. It is not clear why they were awarded an IOH number.

The Naval Uniform Service
15 West 18th Street
New York, NY
(NUS). W
Believe to have been in business during WWII and shortly thereafter only.

Nelson Company
Long Beach, LI, NY. I

The State of New York corporate records show 500 companies with the name Nelson, none as just Nelson Co. located in or near Long Island. One LI company was Nelson Foundry in business from 1943 to 1988 but they made large castings, yet it is possible they made military insignia.

Harry R Newcome & Co.
130 West 42nd St
New York 18, NY

N. R. Newcome & Co.
New York, NY. I

New England Trophy & Engraving Co. IOH N22
Boston, MA. I
Formed on August 1957. They went out of business on 10 January 1979.

Newtel, Inc.
Minneapolis MN
Metal Stampings
It appears they made insignia for foreign countries and swords for USMC.

Niderost & Taber

126 Post Street
San Francisco, CA I

Was incorporated in May 1921 by Joseph H Niderpost and B Taber. No longer in business. They were listed in a directory in the 1950's.

F. H. Noble & Co.

559 W 59th St
Chicago, IL. M

Founded in 1872 by Franklin Noble. Noble was a major manufacturer of findings and jewelry. They made military insignia from WWI through WWII as well as other products. The company was sold (date unknown) and is currently a manufacturer of burial urn vaults. It is a division of Seljan Company in Lake Mills ,WI.

TM Oct 1947, Ser No
71537347

71530553

Ken Nolan Inc.
16901 Milliken
Irvine, CA 92713
210-647-0511

IOH N23N

Established in 2010 as a mail order and catalog company. Does not appear to be in business.

Norsid Mfg
33 Prospect St
Yonkers, NY

IOH 2N

It appears they were in business from WWII until the mid 1960's since they were issued hallmark 2N. It also appears in the 1950's they printed decals, advertising, felt pennants. No information in the 60's.

Norsid pattern for wings in WWII.

The North Attleboro Jewelry Co. IOH N30
112 Bank St
Attleboro, MA 02703
909-599-5035
Founded in 1939 as a manufacturer of emblematic jewelry. Still in business.

Northern Stamping Co. M
No information on this company.

Northeast Emblem & Badge
1853 Peck Ln
Cheshire, CT 06410
203-272-1280
In 2003 this company became part of Waterbury Button Co. which has been in business since 1812 and changed ownership in 2000 to OGS Technologies, Inc.

Northwest Territory Mint IOH N31
Auburn, WA
Founded in 1981 by Ross Hansen, as Auburn Precious Metals and shortly thereafter he began striking silver bullion under the Northwest Territorial Mint brand. The following companies have been acquired by Northwest.
Graco Awards - Current manufacturer of US Military Medals including the MOH. Became a division in 2011.
Medallic Art Company - Founded in 1903 by Henri and Felix Weil. Was the first company to use the Janvier reduction die machine and in 1908 started using the name "Circle of Friends of the Medallion" and very soon afterwards became the Metallic Art Company, in 1910 located at 10 East 17st, New York City. In WWII they manufactured Military Medals.
Military Service Company - Acquired July 2009
Northern Mint- Acquired in 2014.

Nudelman Bros. 1
Portland, OR

Hyman Nudelman opened a butcher shop in downtown Portland and later a small market, but he always wanted to sell clothes. So eventually he opened a haberdashery, where he sold ties and belts, cuff-links and suspenders. His son Eugene joined him in 1926 and they expanded to selling suits, sport coats, and slacks. At first they manufactured most of the clothing they sold, but as the business grew it was less expensive to purchase ready-made clothing.

In the 1930s, the garment unions offered Hyman a contract to supply uniforms for their members, and soon Nudelman Brothers became known throughout the Northwest for its uniforms for streetcar conductors, police, firemen, postal workers and, their largest account, the U.S. Forestry Service. During World War II they also stocked replacement uniforms for sailors.

The Oak Basket   IOH O24
1008 Strengthford Pleasant Rd
Laurel, MS 39440
601-425-4558

Founded in 1984 provides uniforms but primarily operates in the Fund Raising Organizations business.

J. O'Brian Badge Company
Madison, NJ

Officers Equipment Co.(1)
Madison, NJ. (OEC, OEC14-81)

This company was started just after the start of WWII by Mr. Vincent E. Puma and his wife. They operated the business out of their home at 49 Park Avenue, Madison, NJ. Mr. Puma was a jobber, in that he did not manufacture products but rather just sold them and also ran a mail order business. After WWII the business went downhill but sprang back to life in the Korean War. The Puma's passed away in the 1980's. They focused most of their business towards Marines. Most items were not hallmarked. Some of the Paratrooper badges had numbers with the hallmarks these were OEC 15-81 and OEC 14-81. Most of his items were manufactured by V.H. Blackinton & Co.

Officer's Equipment Company (2)   IOH O22

3935 Jefferson Davis Hwy
Stafford, VA 22554-4826
Phone: 703-221-1912

This is not a continuation of the OEC of New Jersey. They are different companies with the same name and basically are the same type of supplier. They manufacturer and sell products related to the USMC. They were incorporated in 1976. Yet they advertise they were established in 1940.

Old Badge Club AKA Andrew Butler Insignia

www.6thJune1944.com

Founded by Andrew Butler a store that operates during summer months near the D-Day beaches in Ste Mere Eglise, France. Also operates outside of Kent UK. In addition to actual items he sell reproduction item. Below is a paratrooper badge he has manufactured.

Olympic Trophy & Awards Co.   IOH O23

5860 North Northwest Highway
Chicago, IL 60639
773-631-9500

Has been in business for approximately 30 making Trophies and recognition items. It appears they have changed there name by dropping the word Olympic.

Oppenstein Brothers Jewelers
Kansas City, MO. I

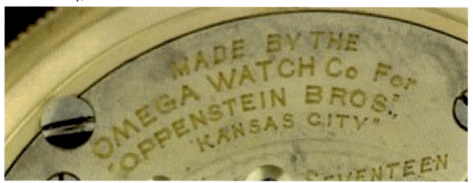

Orber Manufacturing Co.   IOH IO, O1, O21
PO Box 8037
Cranston, RI 02920-0037
401-781-0050

The Orber Manufacturing Company had been in business since 1923 manufacturing jewelry and insignia. They were well known for their police badges and in WWII started making military insignia. Their website is not longer active and it appears they are no longer in business.

Government issue Orber name removed in die.

C. Pacagnini
Milano, Italy. I

Pancraft
Manufacturer of Naval insignia and believed to have started in the 1920's until just after WWII.

Paramount Jewelers
San Francisco, CA . I

Appears to have been in business in the 1920's. Not known when they ceased operations.

Parry & Parry
Salt Lake City, UT. I

No information on this business.

Pasquale Uniform Company   IOH 3P
San Francisco, CA. I, W

Founded in 1854 by Benoit Pasquale, at 103 Fifth Avenue B, then at 115-117 Post St. from 1879 until 1950. All insignia was made under contract by mainly by Blackinton and other eastern manufacturers.

Spanish American War era

WW1

WWII

Patriot Identity   IOH P32
3707 Lockport Rd
Sanborn, NY 14132
312-545-1449
No information on this company.

Patriot Insignia   IOH   P29
287 Knickerbocker Ave
Bohemia, NY 11716
601-425-4558
No information on this company.

Pauls
Buffalo, NY. I
No information on this business.

Paye & Baker Mfg. Co
104 Richards Ave
North Attleboro, MA
Founded in 1896 by as Simmons & Paye, became Paye & Baker (Charles Paye and Frank Baker) in 1901. Went out of business in the 1960s.

Pecas Embroidery Corp.   IOH   P25
1204 67th St
North Bergen, NJ 04047
201-854-1320
Founded in 1981. Federal contracts were found for the years 2005 to 2007. Does not appear to still be in business.

Peerless Embroidery Co.   IOH   P28
2143 North Juniper Lane
Arlington Heights, IL 60004
Established in 1925, has moved to several locations. Current is listed above.

Penn Emblem Co.   IOH P27
10909 Dutton Rd
Philadelphia, PA19154
800-793-7366

In 1947, company founder Frank Blumenthal began embroidering emblems out of his Philadelphia garage to serve the uniform rental market. Still operates as a family business.

E. P. Industries
Providence, Rhode Island
IOH Number P-23
Metal Insignia ceased operations July 2002

Ed Pereia Inc.   IOH P24
Foster, RI.

Personally Yours   IOH P26
115 Charles St
Wenatchee, WA 98801
No information on this business.

Philadelphia Badge Co.
942 Market St.
Philadelphia, PA. I
They made button badges and photo holding badges. This company may have made the photo ID badges. Advertisements have been found as early as 1912. No additional information is known except they were in business during WWII.

Phillips Publications
Owned by Jim Phillips he sold a number of badges mostly paratrooper types. He also had J. Balme make various badges in the 1980's. These badges had a very distinctive designs. It appears he published a number of books, articles on Special Forces activities.

Pichiani-Barlacci
Firenze, Italy

www.picchianiebarlacchi.it
Founded in 1896 by Mr. Gastone Picchiami with a focus on coins and metals. They have minted over 200,000 coins, tokens and metals and are still in operation.

Pichelklammer or Pichlklammer
Innsbruck, Austria
Made some US DIs post war.

Pieces of History   IOH   P30
PO Box 7590
Cave Creek, AZ 85327
Established in 1961 by Mr. Lowell Jackson. In 2010 the business was sold to Sutton Place, LLC. Manufactured reproduction items made overseas.

Carl Poellath
Schrobenhausen, Germany.
(P in a circle)
Carl Poellath Münz- und Prägewerk Schrobenhausen GmbH & Co. KG, Bahnhofstr. 19 - 23, 86529 Schrobenhausen / Germany, Tel. ++49 (0)8252 / 8997-15, www.poellath24.de

The company was founded in 1778 by Johann Christoph Abraham. In 1798 his widow marries Carl Poellath providing the company name. In 1936 they were well known for the manufacturer of the official badges and tags for the Olympic Games in Berlin. After the war they made insignia for US Troops in Europe and in 1978 they changed their official name to GmbH & Co. KG but continue to use the name Poellath.

Thank you for contacting us concerning the paratrooper badges after WWII. We are still producing uniform insignia for German, Norwegian, Republic of Kongo military. After 1945 the American army used the nice villa from our owner as military base in this area Schrobenhausen / Germany. The family had to move in the production facility for that time. A daughter of the owner told me that almost every day a party going on and especially the daughters had a lot of fun over there.

The company Carl Poellath got the order to produce all the military insignia for the US troops based in Europe. This was a big order for the company in this time where a lot of companies were still suffering from the war. Lack of skilled people, damages and so on. I am pretty sure that such parachute badges were produced as well. Unfortunately there no badge anymore left at company but usually Carl Poellath has used the hallmark "C.P." on the badges.

Polar Flight. W
No information is available on this business.

Charles Polk CP

IOH 1P, P21

C. Polk Co./Polk Sales Corp.,
New York, NY. (CP&Co)

There is a great deal of confusion between General Products and Charles Polk. Both appeared to use a very similar hallmark. However General Products was listed as a military metals manufacturer and Charles Polk as an insignia manufacturer.

J. O. Pollack Co.

1700 W Irving Park Rd
Chicago, IL I

Prefax Inc.
IOH P22
509-663-4828
No information on this business.

Preisser
Pforzheim, Germany. I
No information on this concern.

Princeton Industries, Inc.
Providence, RI
No information on this concern.

Rainbow Emblems, Inc.
IOH R25
Johnson, RI. I
No information on this concern.

Rainbow Embroidery
IOH R27
7 Joanna Ct.
East Brunswick, NJ 08816
732-238-9787
www.remiffe.com

Ray Incorporated
IOH R26
5656 Wheatley
Houston, TX 77091
800-322-7824
No information on this concern.

Reed & Barton Silversmiths
The Taunton, Massachusetts, firm of Reed & Barton began in 1824 as Babbitt & Crossman, which produced a cousin of pewter known as Britannia, or Britannia ware. Reed & Barton itself dates to 1840, the same year electroplating was patented in England. By the end of the decade, the company was firmly in the plated-silverware business. In the 1850s and through the Civil War, Reed & Barton sold many of its un-plated pitchers, bowls, and trays to Rogers Bros. of Hartford, Connecticut, which put its hallmark on these plated pieces. Curiously, Reed & Barton bought most of its knives, forks, and spoons from Rogers Bros., which it then plated and stamped as Reed & Barton. During the Civil War, Reed & Barton manufactured weapons for Union troops. Reed & Barton is now part of Lenox.

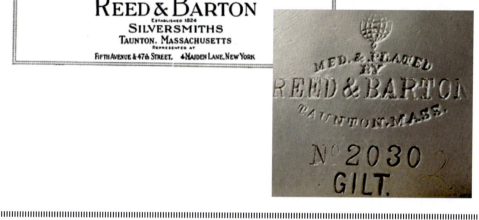

Regal Emblem Co. IOH R23
250 West Broadway Floor 2
New York, NY 10013
(212) 966-1421
I Cage Code: 4T799
Founded in 1931 and currently in business. Recent government contract were for Department of Veterans Affairs for lapel service awards.

Regimental Sign Co. IOH R31
12 Walnut St NW
Washington, DC 20012
202-239-5515
Moved to
PO Box 5319, Takoma Park, MD, 20913
High end sign and memorials as well as insignia and badges.

Reliable World Trade Co., Inc.   IOH A25, T21
9849 KITTY LANE
OAKLAND, CA 94603-1071
(Action Embroidery Corp)
http://www.reliable-world-trade.com/

Rentz Brothers
301 Nicolet Ave
Minneapolis, MN
Based on advertisements an statements of operation they were in business in 1898 to WWI.

Alois Rettenmaier GmbH und Co. KG
Benzholzstraße 16
73525 Schwäbisch Gmünd
Telefon +49 7171 / 92714-0
info@alois-rettenmaier.de
Founded in 1914 and still in business.

Rex Products Corp. M
New Rochelle, NY

Founded in 1902 and remained in business until the end of WWII.

Ad from Dec 4, 1943

The Reynolds Co.   IOH R24
Lincoln, RI. I

No information on this company.

Ricci, Firenze
Italy and Paris France.
Founded in 1932 by Nina Ricci as a fashion design house (haute couture) and during WWII made leather goods. When the war was over they may have made insignia as they returning to fashion and designed bottles, also made custom jewelry.

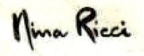

J. W. Richardson & Co.
Providence, RI
Founded in 1852 By J. W. Richardson. It was passed down in the family and with various partners. The last listing in a business listing was 1943 so it is not known when they ceased to exist. Advertisements from the 1920's show them located in New York.

W. R. Richards

RICHARDS, W. E. CO., North Attleboro, MA -- c. 1902 or 1904-2003

The W.E. Richards Company was founded in North Attleboro, MA in 1902 or 1904 and was incorporated in 1907 with Mr. R M Horton as President. They produced WRE and Symmetric costume jewelry of sterling silver with 10K and 14K gold overlay metal with jewelry consisting of Art Deco, Edwardian and Victorian designs using finer high quality materials, cultured pearls, Austrian rhinestones and aurora borealis rhinestone crystals, with some pieces produced containing semi precious stones. The costume jewelry included broaches, rings, scarf and hat pins, links, emblems, and pendants. Mark: "wRe". "Symmetric" since 1936. In 2003 they were purchased by AB Group, parent company of Legère.

Hallmark in use since 1944

Symmetric first used Dec. 1936 - was still being used in 1946.

C. Ridabock & Co.

New York. I
149-151 West 36th Street
New York

Established in 1849 and ceased operations in 1975.

Rixtine
Lincoln, NB. I

Established in 1932 Rixstine Recognition provides a full range of awards, recognition, and promotional items to clients throughout the United States.

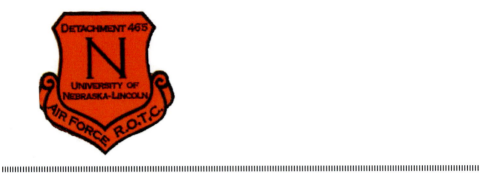

R.K. & Co.
Calcutta, India. I

Charles R. Robbins Company
Robins Co. Inc.

IOH R21

Attleboro, MA
(R in diamond w/wings)
Founded by Charles M. Robbins in Attleboro, Massachusetts in 1892. Began by manufacturing campaign buttons. Ralph Thompson assumed ownership of the company in 1920. In 1912 it was incorporated as Robbins Company, Inc. Acquired by Continental Communications in 1963. They merged with Tharpe Co. in 2007. .

 Post War II

Above WWII

1922 Robbins Co

The Robbins Co.
Attleboro, Mass.

WWI

1904

1890's

Rock Island Arsenal
Rock Island, IL

www.usagria.army.mil

The Rock Island Arsenal comprises 946 acres (383 ha), located on Arsenal Island, originally known as Rock Island, on the Mississippi River between the cities of Davenport, Iowa, and Rock Island, Illinois. It lies within the state of Illinois. The island was originally established as a government site in 1816, with the building of Fort Armstrong. It is now the largest government-owned weapons manufacturing arsenal in the United States.[3] It has manufactured military equipment and ordnance since the 1880s. In 1919–20 one hundred of the Anglo-American or Liberty Mark VIII tanks were manufactured, although too late for World War I. It is designated as a National Historic Landmark.

Established as both an arsenal and a center for the manufacture of leather accouterments and field gear, today it provides manufacturing, logistics, and base support services for the Armed Forces. The Arsenal is the only active U.S. Army foundry, and manufactures ordnance and equipment, including artillery, gun mounts, recoil mechanisms, small arms, aircraft weapons sub-systems, grenade launchers, weapons simulators, and a host of associated components.[4] Some of the Arsenal's most successful products include the M198 and M119 towed howitzers, and the M1A1 gun mount. About 250 military personnel and 6,000 civilians work there.

Rocky Mountain Memorabila   IOH R28
631 Main St
Alamosa, CO 81101
(719) 589-4789
Founded in 2005 and currently operates as gift shop.

Roland I
No information on this concern

Rosenfield Uniform Co
15 School St
Boston, MA. I

Established in 1902 records show it was still in business in the early 1950's. Ads in 1957 are of former employees of this business at the same location with a new name Service Uniform Company.

G. B. Rota
Genoa, Italy (R). I

The Roulet Company
413 Madison Ave
Toledo, OH 43604
419-241-2988   I
http://www.rouletcompany.com

Founded in 1877 and still in operation and owned by the original family.

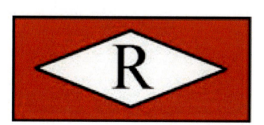

The Rowland Company
Philadelphia, PA. I

Founded by William Rowland. It is believed they were in operation from 1875 to 1920 and may have continued to sell inventory until 1927.

D.J. Ryan Inc   IOH   R22
No information on this concern.

Russell Uniform Co.
192 Lexington Ave
New York 16, NY

Founded around 1891. It is believed they went out of business in the late 1960's when a new Russell Uniform Co was formed in NY in 1968 and supplied uniforms for Broadway shows.

V. Saracino
Taranto, Italy. I
No information available on this company.

I. Scheuer
14 Maiden Ln
New York NY

Sayre Enterprises
Sayre Enterprises, Inc.
P.O. Box 52,45 Natural Bridge School Road
Natural Bridge Station, VA 24579
540-291-3820
www.sayreinc.com

IOH S44

Schreyer Embroidery Co.
50 Industrial Dr.
Fairview, NJ 07022
201-943-6221

It was established in 1956 and appears to still be in business. Categorized under Schiffli Machine Embroideries Manufacturers.

J.M. Schriade
Chicago, IL. I

or

JMS Jewelry Co in business between 1940-and 1960 in Bloomfield, NJ.
or
JMS

Shanholtz Joseph M Jeweler
118 S 8th St
Philadelphia, PA 19107
(215) 627-0911

Various JMS hallmarks have been "guessed" to belong to all three of these companies.

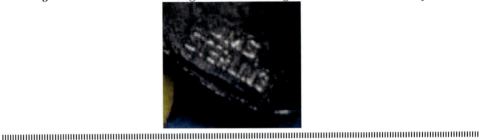

Schwertner & Cie
Graz Eggenberger. I
Schwertner & Cie Nfg GMBH & Co. Kg.
A-8026 Graz
Georgigasse 28 (production)
Georgigasse 40 (Office & Shop)
Austria
Tel .: +43 (0) 316/582 614
Fax .: +43 (0) 316 / 582614-18
info@schwertner.at

Founded in1923 and is now owned by two families Grazer. Werner Reichel and Christian Waldherr lead the company in the 3rd or 4th generation.

Schweizer Emblem Co.

IOH S41

1022 Busse Hwy
Park Ridge, IL 60068
503-659-6984

Established in 1922, it is still a family run business. Patches, coins and emblems.

William Scully Ltd.

2090 Moreau Montreal, QC, Canada H1W 2M3
(514) 527-9333
http://www.williamscully.ca

Founded in 1905 and started to deliever products in 1906. The Canadian military us to this time obtain its insignia from England. Mr. Scully changed the procurement of insignia with his company suppling the Canadian Military. William Scully died in 1921 and the management of the company was passed to his sons, first to Colonel William G. Scully from 1921 to 1947, then to Vincent E. Scully from 1947 to 1957. William G. Scully's son, Vincent G. Scully, is currently president of the firm. During this time other Canadian manufacturers appeared, but Scully has remained in the forefront of the industry in Canada.

Sendai

Sendi is not a hallmark of a company but rather a location. The area is certainly familiar to many American WWII veterans. For some, the memories of Sendai and the Northern Honshu region are not fond ones. In 1944, American POWs were transported in "death ships" to mainland Japan. Those fortunate enough to survive the voyage would spend the remainder of the war in Sendai Division – POW Work Camps. Post World War II, multiple American military installations were set up within the city and surrounding region. Camp Schimmelpfennig would serve as a base for elements of the 1st Cavalry Division. Others would call Camp Sendai home. Just like in Germany the local shops started making items for the rich GI's.

Shops on street outside of Camp Sendai.
Photo by Jim Gregerson 1950's

Shalhoub Brothers   IOH S28
119 West 53rd St
Bayonne, NJ 07002
No information on this business

Joseph M Shanholtz
108 S 8th St
Philadelphia, Pennsylvania 19107-5131
215-627-0911
Also see:
J.M. Schriade
Chicago, IL. I
JMS Jewelry Co
Bloomfield, NJ.
Various JMS hallmarks have been "guessed" to belong to all three of these companies.

Sheridan
14 Florence Street
West Perth
Western Australia 6005
www.sheridans.com.au
1300 313 245
fax +61 (08) 9328 9902

Founded as a small family jewelry shop in 1913 behind the Sheridan family home. The advent of WWI led to a demand for various types insignia and the growth of the company and the formation of the Sheridan's Engraving and Metal Stamping Company. The company is still in business and still owned by the family. During WWII they were known for the manufacturing of US Naval Insignia.

Sherman Manufacturing Co.
Providence, RI.

IOH 3S, S24

///

Shreve & Co.
San Francisco, CA. W

The company was founded in 1854 by George Shreve. By the 1880s, The Shreve Jewelry Company was considered among the finest silversmiths in the United States, selling high quality timepieces, gold, and silver jewelry, aside from diamonds and precious stones. They became Shreve & Co. in 1894 when George Rodman and Albert J. Lewis incorporated the business. It was bought by Schiffman's in November 1992, but they retained its name. Schiffman's is a jewelry concern that started a small jewelry business in Greensboro, NC. in 1893, by Simon Schiffman.

Sherve, Treat & Eacret
San Francisco, CA
Formed in 1912 by Youg George Shreve with Treat and Eacret. Bought by Granat Bros and closed in 1941

Shuttles Bros & Lewis, Inc.
Dallas, TX
Patents dating to 1916 have been found, ceased operation in 1940.

Ben Silver, Inc.
Manhasset, NY. I
Charleston, SC

IOH S30

Started as a coat manufacturer and when President Kennedy swore the Oath of Office without a coat. Coat sales tanked. They then moved to jackets and special buttons reflective of universities, government agencies. The buttons would have the seal of the agency or school. The company is well known for its buttons and clothing lines.

Silverman Brothers / Silverman Corp. IOH S22, 2S
Providence, RI

Silverman Corp that was founded in 1897 or 1898 by Archibald and Charles Silverman. For many years it was known as Silverman Brothers and was in business making jewelry until 1965 or 1966 when Archibald past away. In WWII they made medals and it appears also badges. The hallmark shown has been found on jewelry items to confirm this. For many years it was believe that this hallmark was from a company called Simon Brothers.

They were also assigned the IOH Code 2S. This had been a mystery for a number of years but the timing of when they went out of business would be correct to have this code. This would make sense since they were later issued S22.

Simba Awards, Ltd.
4644 11TH ST
Long Island, NY. 11101
(718) 482-7822

IOH S35

Was founded in 1974 and New York State records indicate it went inactive in 2004.

Simco/E & H Simon Inc.
Do not know when they started fond items from the early 1950's and have found US medals manufactured in late 1960's.

R. F. Simmons Co.
Attleboro, MA

Founded in 1873 by Robert Fitz Simmons who died in 1894 but the business continued. In 1962 they were purchased by Jostens and in 1974 they were purchase by Amtel.

They mainly made watch chains, pins, eyeglass chains and walking stick tops. Use a number of different marks including Armilla, Betsy Ross, Brenda, Floradora, Slident, Stubby, Tyton, Venetian, Victorian, R.F.S. & Co., R.F.S. Co., and Simmons' Chains.

Simon and Sons, Ltd., - SS Ltd
Birmingham, England.

According to the Birmingham Assay Office they were registered in the 1915..1917 time frame as a cigarette case maker. The same name appears in 1898 in the Dublin Assay Office as a manufacturer of FOBs.

Simon Brothers

2438 E. Sergeant Street
P. O. Box 29400
Philadelphia, PA 19125
Phone 1-215-426-9901
Fax 1-215-426-9952
http://www.simonsbrothers.com

The company was founded in 1839 by George Washington Simon and along with his brother P. Bonell Simon. They started to manufacture silver thimbles and pencil cases in gold and silver. During the Civil War they added officer and presentation Swords to their line. Some of the swords were set with gems and etched and engraved and are in the collections of the Pennsylvania Historical Society and the US Naval Academy. In checking with the current company they are not aware of any insignia made by them for the military other than the Swords.

Wm. J. Siravo Designs Inc.   IOH   S43

101 Comstock Parkway Unit 13
Cranston, RI 02921
NCAGE 05GF3
The company was founded in 1995 and closed it doors in 2003.

N.G. Slater Corp.   IOH   S31

42 W 38th St #1002,
New York, NY, 10018   I
(212) 768-9434
N.G. Slater was founded in 1936 by Nathaniel George Slater as a specialist in "Lithographed Metal Advertising Buttons and Tabs". Still in business offering promotional imprinted items.

Daniel Smilo & Sons

304-320 E 45St
New York,17 NY. M
Approximate dates of operation WWII to Vietnam Era.

Smart Design Inc IOH S50
833 Highams Ct
Woodridge, VA 22191
914-948-4619
www.smartdesigninc.com

Established as a sole-proprietorship in 1995. Since then, Smart Design has incorporated and continues to be a small, woman-owned, veteran-owned business in the Washington, DC metro area. Authorized to manufacture plaques.

Smith And Warren
127 OAKLEY AVENUE
WHITE PLAINS,NY
914-948-4619
www.smithwarren.com

Manufacturer of badges and uniform insignia since 1925.

IOH S50

Snag-Prufe Fasteners
PO BOX 36351
Louisville, KY 40233-6351

IOH S25

Spies Brothers, Inc.
27 E. Monroe St.
Chicago, IL. I

No history can be found but based on articles and advertisements for class rings and award pendants this company was established in 1878 and ceased production after WWII.

Spink and Son Ltd.

5-7 King Street, St James
London SW1
United Kingdom

Spink was established in 1666 as a firm of silversmiths. In 1880 we entered the Medal business with the purchase of the Soho Mint and in 1897 produced the commemorative medals for Queen Victoria's Diamond Jubilee, being awarded the Royal Warrant in 1900. We still retain this Warrant and are Royal Medalists to HM Queen Elizabeth II, HRH The Duke of Edinburgh, and HRH The Prince of Wales. Their archives were destroyed by a bomb during World Wars II.

Sports Caddy LLC   IOH S45

1801-J Crossbem Dr.
Charlotte, NC 28217
502-458-2769

Was established in 1994. No longer in business.
US Trademark 75415525. Canceled in 2005.

SPORTS CADDY

Stabilimenti Artistici

Pratese Street 40 / A, 50145
Florence, Italy

Stadri Emblems Inc.   IOH   S42
1760 Glasco Turnpike
Woodstock, NY 12498
A family owned business started in 1955, became incorporated in 1984 still in operation.

Standard Manufacturing Co.   IOH   S23
Several companies have this same name but none appeared to be in the insignia business.

Starcrest
Made insignia in WWII but normally produced women's jewelry. Then made for collector and veterans items.

Sta-Bright Products   IOH   S39
3300 Clipper Mill Rd
Baltimore, MD 21211
Mame Trademark 1990 for military insignia serial number 74101933 by HENRY E. FRIEDLANDER UNIFORMS & INSIGNIA, INC. and is still active. This company was established in 1984 and is the parent company of Sta-Bright. The Trademark is now owned by Ira Green Co.

Stay Sharp Tool Co. Inc. IOH S34
PO Box 1069
229 West St
North Attleboro, MA 02760
Was established in 1973 and was a metal stamping co. No longer in business.

Stefano Johnson
Milan, Italy

Italian company of medalists, founded in 1836 by Stefano Johnson. In that year he struck his first medal in the Milanese workshop of his father, Giacomo Johnson, who had recently moved from Birmingham after a brief period of activity in Lyon. The production of medals and plaques received an important stimulus from Stefano's son Federico Johnson, who employed medalists from the Mint in Milan, which had closed in 1887. Having obtained the services of several well-known sculptors, Federico began producing medals to commemorate historical and religious events and every aspect of Italian industrial, commercial and financial activity. The company's products also began to be exported by his son Stefano Johnson II and his grandson Cesare Johnson. Following the destruction of the workshop in air-raids in 1943, Cesare built new premises in Milan. He also increased the cultural status of medals by publishing the magazine Medalist in collaboration with his wife, Velia Johnson, and by cataloging the company's collection of c. 50,000 medals, which is readily accessible to scholars. The company produced medals in collaboration with such major Italian sculptors as Emilio Greco, Luciano Minguzzi, E. Fazzini, F. Bodini, E. Manfrini, Arnaldo Pomodoro and V. Crocetti. In the late 20th century work continued under the guidance of Riccardo Johnson, Mariangela Johnson and her husband, Roberto Pasqualetti.

Stempel-Schutz I
Roswitha Schulz
Heidelberger Str. 127
PLZ / Ort
64285 Darmstadt
Telefon 06151 96680
http://www.stempel-schulz.de

Louis Stern Co.
Providence, RI

They were formed in 1871 as a chain makers and silversmiths. Last known to be in business 1950. During the war years was known for large art-deco designs.

Lapel Pin

They used a number of hallmarks as listed here:
Wristacrat -- 1924
Waite-Evans
W.E.
Dainty Maid
Glamour
L.S.CO.
L.S.
Y. & S.
E.P.H.
L.S. & CO.
Little Flower Rosary
Presit

Stitch Gallery Inc.   IOH S48
113 S 77 Sunshine Strip
Harlingen, TX 78550

Established in 1994 by Eduardo and Dolma A. Diaz. Embroidery and screening of products. Still in business.

Stitchen Post

IOH S49

1649 1ST St E.
Bradenton, FL 34208 212-924-3133
Custom embroidery store that was established in 2004 and still in operation.

Stokes - Stokes & Sons - Thomas Stokes & Sons

Unit 1, 2 Jindalee Place
Riverwood NSW 2210
Australia

Stokes was established in 1856 by a young English die-sinker named Thomas Stokes, who had arrived from England some years earlier to take part in the gold rush of that era. Disappointment in the fields led him to Melbourne where he setup business as a die-sinker producing medals, tokens, buttons and silverware, a skill he acquired over five dedicated years of apprenticeship which he had completed in Birmingham, England. A merger with G.F Martin in 1867 saw the firm introduce electroplated nickel silver to Australia. The banking crisis of the 1890's saw a split with Martin and the gradual joining of Thomas Stokes' three sons, and by 1911 the company was called Thomas Stokes and Sons. The company's pre-eminent status amongst its competitors was demonstrated by the commission to produce Queen Elizabeth ll's wedding gift from Australia and her 1954 tour gift from Victoria.

Franz Sturies

Germany. I
No information on this concern.

Sugerman also
Harry Sugerman Company

IOH S21

also used the marks Susco
Harry first use of his mark SUSCO according to the US Patent office was 1950 and it expired sometime shortly after 1986.
Harry Sugerman, Inc. 1116 E. Houston St. San Antonio TX

Sun Badge Co.

IOH S47

712 W Cierega Ave
San Diams, CA 91773
201-953-6221
Established in 2010 and is currently a nondurable good wholesaler.

Superior Die & Stamping Inc.

IOH S46

9 Newbury St
Norton, MA 02766
774-203-3674
Established in 1978. Currently in business has no hallmark that they use.

Supreme Military Insignia

IOH S26

No information on this business.

The Supply Room, Inc.

IOH S38

230 Supply Room Rd
Oxford, AL 36203
(256) 835-7676
800-458-5180
www.supplyroom.com

Sussman. I
No information on this concern.

Sutton Mfg.

IOH S37

28 Sutton Ave
East Providence, RI 02914
No information on this business. Address is for a small single family home.

Swank, Inc.
Attleboro, MA. M
Swank was founded in 1897 focusing in mens jewelry and accessories. The company was acquired by Randa Accessories in 2012.

J. J. Sweeney Jewelry Co.
419 Man corner of Preston
Houston, TX
Founded in 1875 and creased operations in 1963. During WWI they offered their manufacturing facilities to the US Government. They were involved in repair and overhaul of ships chronometers and watches for the US Shipping Board. They also made the

Bombardier Wing and applied for a patent for its design which was awarded in 1922. The wing was designed by Henri Marvet, Patent number 61445.

Swiss Maid Inc.   IOH   S40
RDI #1, Mozzette Rd
Greentown, PA 18426
No information on this company.

Swiss-Tex Corp.
IOH S29

No information on this company.

Swift & Fisher
IOH S17

North Attleboro, MA
(Harry W. Fisher and Joseph H. Swift)
Believed to have been in business from 1913 through 1965.

Trademark was issued in 1944,
Reg number 71470641
It expired in 1986

A set of three paratrooper badges may
be the only items with this hallmark

S- Unknown WWI era style wing

O.C. Tanner Company

1930 S. State Street
Salt Lake City, UT 84115
(800) 453-7490
www.octanner.com

The company was formed by Obert C. Tanner in 1927 selling graduation class rings and pins. After WWII they started selling corporate recognition awards and this is the current business model with worldwide sales and 1500 employees. In 1954 they build there first factory which means military items prior to 1954 were made by other companies under contract. CTO was trademarked serial number 72116763. now expired.

T&P. 1
No information on this company.

Taxco
Taxco, Mexico

Taxco de Alarcón (Taxco) is a small city and administrative center of a municipality of the same name (Taxco de Alarcón) located in the Mexican state of Guerrero. This is an area known for silver mines and other metals and for the crafting of it into jewelry and silverware. Many of the stores in the town sell locally produced silver items.

A&S Taub   IOH T23
17610 Northeast 8th Place
Bellevue, WA 98009
425-644-7874
Sign Manufacturer also engraving. Does not appear to be in business.

TC Art & Craft Works   IOH T22
6777 Hawaiiki Dr
Honolulu, HI 96825
No information on this company.

Telepunch Inc.   IOH T25
524 Echo Ln
Palatine, IL 60067
Believed to have been formed in 1991 but no other records exist.

Teh Ling
Yohamma?, Japan

Belt Buckle 1 x 2 inches

Thomas Co.
Attleboro, MA.
No information on this company.

Thomas Fattorini, Ltd
Regent Street Works
Birmingham B1 3HQ
United Kingdom
tel. +44 (121) 236 1307
http://www.fattorini.co.uk

The company was founded in 1827 by Antonio Fattorini an Italian speaking immigrant who settled in Yorkshire where he established a number of retail outlets specializing in jewelry, watches and fancy goods including barometers.

Tiffany & Co. Inc.
New York, NY

The firm was founded by Charles L. Tiffany in 1837 with John B. Young under the name Tiffany & Young.

In 1851 John C. Moore & Son entered into a special business relationship with Tiffany.

In 1868 the silverware factory of Moore became part of organization with Edward C. Moore becoming one of the directors.

Throughout the remaining years of the 19th century, Tiffany's won wide acclaim for the nature of its product and the wealth of its clientele.

Tiffany and Co. moved to its current location on New York 5th Ave. in 1940. The new building was immensely beautiful and was designed in the art deco style. Above the door is a statue of Atlas bearing the weight of the world. Instead of a globe being held above his head, he holds a clock. The architects of the building wanted to create an ominous affect that reminded Tiffany & Co.'s visitors of the rarity and preciousness of the treasures carried by the store. For that reason, all of the buildings doors were made to look like the doors of industrial bank vaults.

Today, Tiffany & Co. remains a leading maker of jewelry, china, crystal, silver, and glassware. Tiffany's sterling pieces are some of the purest to be found in the world.

WWI Navy Pilot Wing

Tommy Tucker T-Shirts   IOH T24

930 North Stone Avenue
Tucson, AZ 85705
520-325-7782
Formed in 1924 with its primary business is the manufacture of T-shirts with both embroidery and screening. Both wholesale and retail.

Truart - Tru Art Jewelry Co., Inc
50 Aleppo St
Providence, RI
Known for its art pieces with a 1940's style. Believed to have creased operations in the mid 1960's. Made WWII Sweetheart items.

Tucker Shean
1123 "O" Street
Lincoln, NB. I
Jewelers around the 1900's founded by C A Tucker who was a jeweler and Dr. S. S. Shean who was an optician. Records show they were in business in the 1930's it is not known when they ceased operations.

Uncas Manufacturing Company, Inc

150 Niantic Avenue
Providence, RI 02907
401.944.4700

Established in 1911 by Vincent Sorrentino under his name and in the early 1920's the name changed to Uncas. In 1998 they purchased Vargas Manufacturing Co. and moved to the Vargas factory. They are still in business and are now a world wide organization.

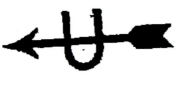

Hallmark registered 1/21/1922

Hallmark registered 12/20/1947

Hallmark registered 12/20/1947

United Emblem Co.

3956 63rd St
Woodside, NY 11377-3649
(212) 962-3869
Paul Liebold- Owner
Manufacturer of metal products including emblems and medals.

United Insignia Company Inc.
397 Bridge Street
Brooklyn, NY 11201
http://www.unitedinsignia.com/
(718) 222-3400
Formed during WWII and still in business. Currently manufacturers police and fire badges.

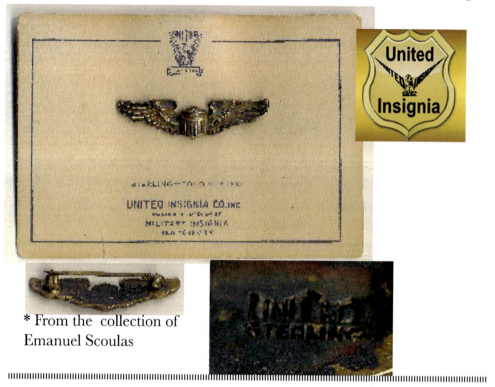

* From the collection of Emanuel Scoulas

United Military
New York, NY. I

IOH 6U

No information on this company.

United States Government
Only two US Government locations are known to have manufactured insignia the first is Rock Island Arsenal (see their listing) and the second is the US Mint in Philadelphia, PA. Only a few known wings were made in the 1920's and are marked "FROM OFFICIAL DIE." The die would be loaned to insignia manufactures.

United Uniform Accessories Inc.   IOH U22
30-30 Northern Blvd
Long Island City, NY 11101
No longer in business. No information on this company.

Universal Specialty Awards
AKA - The Providence Mint
1205 Westminister St
Providence, RI 02909
401-727-0083
www.tpm-usa.net
The two above listed companies merged in 2004. Authorized to manufacture medals and Distinctive Unit Insignias but does not have an IOH number.

Uris Sales Corp   IOH 4U
URISCRAF
222 Fourth Ave
New York, 3 NY
1931 - 1967

Made insignia and sweetheart jewelry in WWII. This hallmark came off a 2 9/16 inch pilot wing. which may have been aimed at the sweetheart market since it is an odd size. The hallmark in the red picture came off a WWII Paratrooper wing. After the war they made merchandise for Post Exchanges and appeared to cease in the mid to late 1960's.

Urschel Tool Corp.

IOH U21

Cranston, RI. I
Established in 1948 and still in business.

U.S. Infantry Association
Washington, DC. I
No current association by this name.

U.S. Specialty Co.
New York, NY. I
No information on this business.

A. Valcan
Japan I
This company is currently listed as a toy manufacturer. They were known for military and "tin" toy robots.

W. A. Valdez
Philippines I
No information on this business.

Vanalen Company
New York, NY and Kansas City, MO. I
No information on this company.

Vanguard Military Equip. Co/Vanguard Insignia Co.

IOH 1V, V-21, V-21-N, After 2000 M-22

Brooklyn/NYC/Norfolk, VA/Carlsbad, CA.

Founded in New York City in 1918 by Bernard Gershen who arrived in the US in 1903 he was tailor and found work at NY Sea Ports sewing. Working right on the piers, Bernard soon began to specialize in sewing the gold lace onto the jackets of the ship's captain and crew. At the end of WWI, in 1918, a gentleman by the name of Sam Weisberg, whose business was selling buttons to Navy personnel located at the Brooklyn Navy Yard, approached him with the idea of forming their own company. Mr. Weisberg would specialize in buttons and other metal items, and Bernard would specialize in lace and other sewn items.

While the name Vanguard has significant meaning to all of us now, these gentlemen decided they had to pick a name for their company. What they did was simply open the dictionary and point to a word at random. They agreed that if they both knew what the word meant, that would be their company name. Obviously, they flicked the book open to the back where the V's are found, and Vanguard was born. From this small beginning, Vanguard had a very modest and meager start, and up until the onset of WWII in 1941, there were no more than 10 employees, including the two partners, at any one time. With the dramatic growth of the armed forces of WWII, Vanguard marched steadily forward, and began to grow in 1965 into the largest manufacturer of insignia in the USA. In 1985 they merged with Wolf Brown, Inc which resulted in opening a west coast factory and in 2000 they purchased the remaining assets of N S Meyer. Today they are one of the few insignia manufacturers left.

Van Wormer & Rodrigues
126 Post Street Rm. 300,
San Francisco, CA. I
Founded on May 6, 1929. The company is no longer in business.

Vargas Manufacturing Company
150 Niantic Ave
Providence, RI
1945 - about 1996 when they were purchased by Uncas Manufacturing. However they ceased operations around 1980. Their primary focus was ornamental costume jewelry. Horizontal diamond with superimposed "V". First used in 1947.

Volupte, Inc.
Elizabeth, NJ

Volupte was founded in the 1920's in Elizabeth, NJ as a manufacturer of compacts and cigarette cases. They also made jewelry using a chromium-plated metal mesh.
Bought by Shields, Inc., Attleboro, MA in 1957 and ceased operations in the 1960's.
Shields was founded in 1920 as the Fillkwik Co and in 1936 changed it's name to Shields, Inc. In 1939 it was purchased by Rex Products, New Rochelle, NY, which is well known as a medal manufacturer. In 1957 they purchased Volupte, Inc. of Elizabeth, NJ another medal manufacturer. The hallmark of V in a circle can be found on a number of US medals.

Voyager Emblems
IOH V22
3707 Lockport Rd
Sanborn, NY 14132
716-731-4121
Founded in 1967 they are a full service embroidery company. Still in operation.

Vulcan
Tokyo, Japan
("AT" in heart). I
No information on this business, this may be the company under the name A. Valcan.

Vulcan Industries
IOH V22
Birmingham, AL.
Founded in 1946 and may have shipped items under the name of Military Service Company (MSC). Both of these companies are now a division of EBSCO Industries.

Wall & Dougherty
Honolulu, HI
Established on April 1, 1912 by Arthur Wall and James Donahue Dougherty. Records show the business was still in being in 1925. No other information was found.

Wallace Bishop Co.
Brisbane, Australia
This firm was founded in 1917 and has been in the same family ever since and is still in operation. The badge making arm was phased out towards the late 1990's due to the flood of Asian imports onto the Australian market.

The Wallace Co., Inc.   IOH 2W
Providence, RI.
The company was founded in 1944 and dissolved in November 1991.

C.H. Wallbank Company
312 Spring St
Brookline, MA 02132
617-323-8562
Founded in 1931 and appears to still be in business more in the retail trade of jewelry.

chWco
STERLING

Wallenstein I
No information on this business.

Warner Woven Label Company Inc   IOH W24
500 E 35th St
Paterson, NJ 07504
The company was founded in 1903 in Paterson, NJ. At it's peak it was one of the largest woven label companies in the world. Their sales office was located at 111 W. 40th Street, New York, New York. It ceased operation in 1994.

Warwick Emblem Supply

IOH W30

141 Inez Ave
Warwick, RI 02886
401-738-0702

Established in 1992, but currently shows only one employee the owner Elaine Warwick.

Waterbury Companies, Inc. M

Founded in 1812 by Aaron Benedict and they have been making buttons every since and to this day. To see more back codes for the buttons go to:

http://www.waterburybutton.com/cart/pc/viewContent.asp?idpage=5

Would call your attention to our new line of Military Sash and Collar Pins. Orders filled promptly from stock at our New York Store.

WATERBURY BUTTON CO.
48 HOWARD STREET NEW YORK   WATERBURY, CONN.

Wehing Brothers Mfg.
Detroit, MI

This is listed in some documents but is a mis-spelling of Weyhing Brothers Mfg.

Weidmann
Frankfurt, Germany. I

No information on this company.

Weingarten Gallery

IOH W32

14066 Deer Stone Ln
Fishers, IN 46040
www.1903.com
317-598-1026

In 1968 Joe Weingarten and his wife started to manufacture hand made jewelry. Joe was commissioned in the Air Force and stationed at Wright-Patterson in the Airdrop and Air Cargo Research and Development Branch with extra time in the evenings. In 1971 he left the service but continue to work at Wright Patterson in the same branch as a Civil Service an aerospace engineer. He obtained 11 US Patents including one for the manufacturer of castings. When the Hunt Brothers caused a silver crisis he was asked by the Air Force Museum head if he could make aircraft charms as the gift shop was not longer able to get them. That was the start of over 450 different aircraft charms and tie tacks. In 1998 Joe retired, after almost 30 years of service, as the Technical Assistant to the Commander of the Air Force Material Command, and started full time making reproduction insignia and current insignia. (See back cover) After 40 years in Dayton, OH he moved to Fishers, IN. Currently Weingarten Gallery is the only source for many current insignia in sterling silver in the US. www.1903.com. In 2008 Weingarten Gallery obtained the legal rights to the Luxenberg Hallmark. Products are manufactured under two trademarks IOH mark W32 and Luxenberg.

Wellington

Tokyo, Japan. I

Wendell & Co.
618 W. Jackson St
Chicago, IL. I

Originally formed in 1885 by Maurice Wendell as Wendell & Co., manufacturing jewelers. The last know record of this company was in 1943.

1922

1900

Wright Brothers souvenir medal. Not know if this is the same company. Circa 1910.

Wendwll's Inc.   IOH W31
6601 Industry Ave
Ramey MN 55303

Founded in 1882 manufacturing rubber stamps, stencils and steel engraving for local industry. Today they are custom mint and also make stamps as they did when the company started.

Western Military Supply Co.   IOH 11W, W23
Japan/San Francisco, CA. (11W, W23)
203-597-1812

This company was AKA -Konwal.

Weyhing Brothers Manufacturing Company,
3040 Gratiot Ave
Detroit, MI
(313) 567-0600

Founded in 1903 and was in business until it was purchased by Smith & Warren in 2014. All dies have been transferred to the new owners in White Plains, N.Y, ending the over 100 years of making badges and insignia in Detroit. It appears this unique screw back paratrooper badge is the only military badge they made.

Whitehead and Hoag
Newark, NJ. ("WH" in a shield) I, M, W

The partnership of Whitehead (Benjamin S. Whitehead) and Hoag (Chester R. Hoag) was formed in 1892 and soon to became the country's largest business in the manufacture of advertising novelties. In May, 1959 the company was purchased by Bastian Bros. and they used the WH name until it was phased out in 1964-65.

1918

H. H. P. Whittemore and Co
Attleboro, MA.
Sweetheart jewelry during WWII.

217

H F Wichman & Co.
Honolulu, HI. 96813
(808) 942-4858
Founded by Henry F. Wichman in the late 1800's. Still in business as a retail jewelry store.

Wick Embroidery Co
IOH W26
208-36TH STREET
UNION CITY, NJ 07087
201-864-4827
Established: 1/6/1976
Cage Number 6M572
Last Government contract was in 2000.

F.M. Wickham. I
No information on this business.

Wil-Tex Industries
IOH W28
377 Pacific St
Paterson, NJ 07503
401-738-0702
No information on this company.

Williams & Anderson, Co.
IOH W25
North Main & Third St
Providence, RI
This company was established in 1901. In 1934 they Trademarked the diamond hallmark and it expired in 2005. It was last renewed in 1994. Serial Number 71347429. They were bought out by Barrows Industries, Inc., and it appears they have ceased operations.

1922 Hallmark

Korean era

Vietnam Era - W25

Windsor Gramercy Corp. IOH W29
55 W 39th St
New York, NY 10018
(212) 302-5180
No information of what they made for the military currently sell New York real estate.

C.A. Winship
7S State St
Chicago, IL
It appears they were in business as early as 1890 from an advertisement and from this pin into the 1940's. Unable to find any other records.

Wolf Appleton Co.
556 Broadway
New York, NY
A patch manufacturer, I have found references to this company from 1955 to mid 1960's. In addition to military they were a major Boy Scout patch maker.

Wolf-Brown, Inc.   IOH W22
Los Angeles, CA
I have found references to Wolf-Brown in the manufacturer of Shriners Hats from the mid 1950's to the 1970's. In addition I have found pictures of DI's.
In 1985, Vanguard expanded to both coasts when it merged with the Wolf-Brown Corporation

Brown-Wolf hallmark found on a sword, made in Germany

J. R. Wood Products Corp.
New York, NY
Founded in 1850 by J. R. Wood in Brooklyn NY. They were engaged mainly in ring production and not military. Many of their items were sold under the Artcarved name and others. It appears that during WWII they entered into war production and made metals. In 1970 they merged into Leonx, Inc and in 1975 the name was changed to Art-Carved.

     1920's Hallmark

World Merchandise Co
536 Broadway
New York, NY

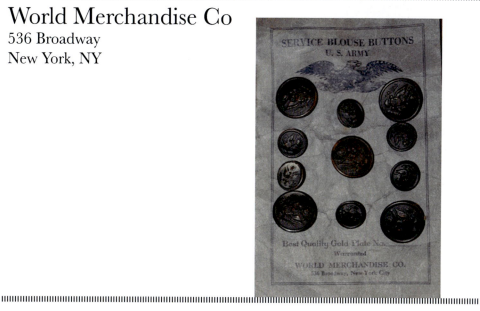

Wright and Street
Chicago, IL.
Earliest documentation is from 1915 and latest during WWII. It is not know when they ceased operations.

Weyersberg, Kirschbaum & Co
Solingen, Germany

Has been manufacturing swords since 1774. The company was founded by the Weyersberg's and in 1883 they merged with the Kirschbaums. They made US Military swords for all branches.

6W - unknown

Yorktowne Sports Inc.
74 Cranbrook Rd
Cockeysville, MD 21030
410-569-9009.

A store front business offering embroidering and screen printing. Currently in business.

G & T Young aka Young & Co.
Auckland, New Zealand

The store, which opened in 1862, was believed to be New Zealand's oldest jewelery business. The business ceased to exist 27 January 2009 when it was liquidated by court order. It appears that during WWII they made some US Military insignia for people stationed in New Zealand.

Crispulo Zamora
Manila, Philippines

Crispulo de Mendoza Zamora (10 June 1871 – 11 October 1922) was a silversmith and, during his time, was considered the best engraver in the country. On 10 June 1892, Zamora married Pelagia Mendoza by whom he had seven children, namely, Angel, Juan, Rosario, Vicente, Clemente, Eduardo, and Esperanza. His wife continued operating his engraving business after his death. When his wife died on 13 March 1939, his children took over the business. From then on, his shop became known as Crispulo Zamora Sons.

Zart's Inc.   IOH   Z21
155 Moshassuck St
Pawtucket, RI 02860
It is believed this company was formed on June 6, 1983 and is no longer active.

Appendix A

Over the next several pages are the cover sheets for various jewelry patents if you wish more information just Google the patent number or go to the US Patent and Trademark office at http://patft.uspto.gov/ or http://www.uspto.gov/patents-application-process/search-patents

Jan. 12, 1943. F. A. BALLOU, JR., ET AL 2,308,412
SECURING DEVICE
Filed May 13, 1942

INVENTOR
Frederick A. Ballou Jr.
Melvin W. Moore
BY
ATTORNEYS

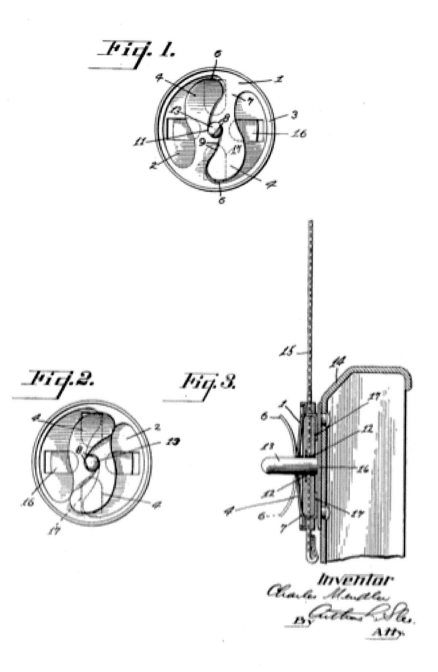

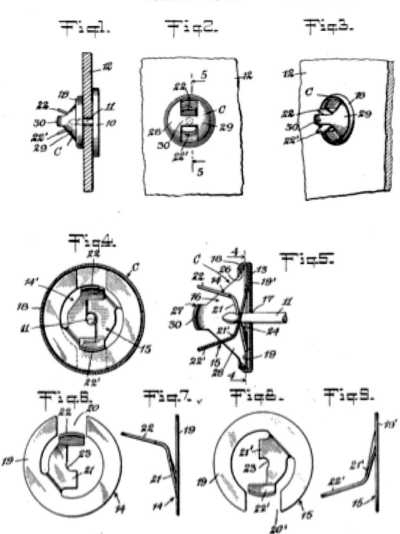

Appendix B

Pre and WWII German Party badges hallmarks. These are the assigned ID Numbers for manufactures of NAZI party badges. The prefix M1/ has been left out. So each hallmark would be M1/number

1-Kallenbach,Meyer & Franke-Luckenwalde.
2-Richard, Conrad-Weimar.
3-Max, Kremhelmer-Munchen.
4-Karl, Gutenkunst-Oranienburg.
5-Walter,Simon-Dresden.
6-Karl, Hensler-Pforzheim.
7-Herman, Schanzlin-Pforzheim.
8-Ferdinand, Wagner-Pforzheim.
9-Robert, Hauschild-Pforzheim.
10-Robert, Schenkel-Pforzheim.
11-C, Balmberger-Nurmberg.
12-Gebruder, Hahne-Ludenscheid.
13-L, Christian Lauer-Nurmberg.
14-Matthias, Oechsler & Sohne-Ansbach.
15-Ferdinand, Hoffstatter-Bonn.
16-Franke & Co-Ludenscheid.
17-Assmann & Sohne-Ludenscheid.
18-Gold, & Silberschmiede Anstalt-Oberstein.
19-Unknown.
20-Gustav,Emil Ficker-Beirfeld.
21-Paul, Meybauer-Berlin.
22-Johann, Dittrich-Cheminitz.
23-Wilhelm, Borgas-Eutingen.
24-Overhoff & Cie-Ludenscheid.
25-Rudolf, Reiling-Pforzheim.
26-Unknown.
27-E.L. Muller-Pforzheim.
28-Gebruder, Traulz-Pforzheim.
29-Otto, Riedel-Zwickau.
30-Robert, Metzger-Pforzheim.
31-Karl, Pfohl-Pforzheim.
32-Gustav, Ramminger-Pforzheim.
33-Unknown.
34-Karl, Wurster-Markneukirchen.
35-Wachtler & Lange-Mittweida.
36-Berg & Nolte-Ludenscheid.
37-Julius, Bauer Sohne-Zella-Mehlis.
38-Carl Wachtler-Weimar.
39-Robert, Beck-Pforzheim.
40-Meinel & Scholer-Klingenthal.
41-H.A. Kohlers Sohne-Altenburg.
42-Kerbach & Israel-Dresden.
43-Julius, Maurer-Oberstein a.d.n
. 44-C. Dinsel-Berlin. 45-Friedrich, Linden-Ludenscheid.
46-Alfred, Stubbe-Berlin.
47-Christain, Dicke-Ludenscheid.
48-Alexander Wollram-Dessau.
49-Adolf, Baumeister-Ludenscheid.
50-Richard, Sieper & Sohne-Ludenscheid.
51-Noelle & Hueck-Ludenscheid.
52-Deschler & Sohne-Munchen.
53-Grebruder, Wegerhoff-Ludenscheid.
54-F.A. Fries, Beuster & Schild-Berlin.
55-August, Enders-Oberrahmede.
56-Erfurter, Knopffabrik-Erfurt.
57-M. Winter-Munchen.
58-M Kutsch-Attendorn.
59-Paul, Cramer-Ludenscheid.
60-Grebruder, Cosack-Neheim.
61-Ossenberg-Engels-Iserlohn.
62-Gustav, Hahl-Pforzheim.
63-Steinhauer & Luck-Ludenscheid.
64-Albert Winges-Trusen.
65-Weidmann-Frankfurt am Main.
66-Fritz Kohm-Pforzheim.
67-Karl, Schenker-Schwab-Gmund.
68Gustav Maier-Pforzheim.
69-Unknown.
70-Franz Otto -Wuppertal/Elberfeld.
71-Gasell & Co-Pforzheim.
72-Fritz Zimmermann-Stuttgart.
73-Karl, Erbacher-Pforzheim.
74-Boerger & Co-Berlin.
75-Otto Schickle-Pforzheim.
76-Hillebrand & Boer-Ludenscheid.
77-Foerster & Barth-Pforzheim.
78-Paulmann & Crone-Ludenscheid.
79-Walter, Umlauf-Leipzig.
80-R. Durr & Fr Seiter-Pforzheim.
81-Rutting & Mertz-Ludenscheid.
82-Leistner & Co-Leipzig.
83-Willy, Annetsberger-Munchen.
84-Ernst, Schneider-Ludenscheid.
85-Alois, Rettenmaier-Schwab-Gmund.
86-Ernst, Cronze-Ludenscheid.
87-Karoline, Gahr-Munchen.

88-Josef, Schulte/Ufer-Sundern.
89-Gustav, Buhnert-Dobein.
90-Apreck & Vrage-Leipzig.
91-Unknown.
92-Carl,Wild-Hamburg.
93Gottlieb, Fredrich Keck & Sohne-Pforzheim.
94-Fredrich, Keck-Pforzheim.
95-Josef, Fuess-Munchen.
96-F.O. Naupert-Rosswein.
97-M. Nett Gravier & Prageanstalt-Furth.
98-G. Danner-Muhlhausen.
99-Peter Wilhelm Heb-Ludenscheid.
100-Werner, Redo-Saarlautern.
101-Gustav,Brehmer-Markneukirchen.
102-Frank & Reif-Stuttgart-Zuffenhausen.
103-Carl, Poellath-Schrobenhausen.
104-Otto, Fechler-Bernsbach.
105-Hermann, Aurich-Dresden.
106-Funcke & Bruninghaus-Ludenscheid.
107-Emil, Juttner-Ludenscheid.
108-Wilhelm, Schroder & Co-Ludenscheid.
109-Glaser & Sohne-Dresden.
110-Tweer & Turck-Ludenscheid.
111-Gebruder, Gloerfeld Metallwarenfabrik-Ludenscheid.
112-Robert, Deitenbeck-Ludenscheid.
113-Gebruder, Dornbach-Ludenscheid.
114-Paul, Cramer & Co-Ludenscheid.
115-E.Schmidhaussler-Pforzheim.
116-Hermann. Wernstein-Jena/Lobstadt.
117-K.F..Vogelsang & Co-Ludenscheid.
118- Erich. Gutenkunst-Berlin.
119-Georg. Bonitz-Schwarzenberg.
120-Wilhelm. Deumer-Ludenscheid.
121-Walter. Demmer-Ludenscheid.
122-I.Deutschbein-Euuskirchen.
123-Petz & Koch-Unter Reichenbach.
124-Gebruder.Lange-Ludenscheid.
125-Cramer & Dombach-Ludenscheid.
126-Karl.Fredrich Schenkel-Pforzheim.
127-Alfred.Stbbe, Inhaber Herbert Tegge-Berlin/Waidmannslust.
128-Eugen.Schmidhaussler-Pforzheim.
Post 1939
129-Seller & Co-Geldern.
130-Grossmann & Co Inhaber Lorenz Hoffstatter & L.Siefener-Wien.
131-to-135-Unknown.(Reserved for Austrian Makers but never registered).
136-Mathias.Salcher & Sohne-Wagstadt.
137-Richard.Simm & Sohne-Gablonz a.d.n.
138-Mathias.Oechsler & Sohne-Riegersdoft/Bodenbach.
139-Rudolf.Richter-Schlag.
140-Bruno.Czerch-Gablonz a.d.n.
141-Josef.Feix & Sohne-Gablonz a.d.n.
142-Josef.Hillerbrand-Gablonz a.d.n.
143-Gebruder,Jager-Gablonz a.d.n.
144-Unknown.
145-Unknown.
146-Anton.Schenkels Nachfolger-Wien.
147-Eduard Gosel-Wien.
148-Heinrich.Ulbrichts Witwe-Wien.
149-Lentwerk Bruder Schneider-Wien.
150-Franke & Sohne-Heidenreichstein..d.n.
151-Rudolf.Schanes-Wien.
152-Franz Jungwirth-Wien.
153-Fredrich Orth-Wien.
154-Unknown.
155-Schwertner & Cie-Eggenberg bei Graz.
156-Argentor Werke-Wien.
157-Phillip Turks Witwe-Wien.
158-Karl Pichl-Innsbruck.
159-Hanns Doppler-Wels.
160-E Reihl-Linz.
161-Anton Markovskys & Sohne-Gablonz a.d.n.
162-Konrad Seiboth-Gablonz a.d.n.
163-Franz Schmidt-Gablonz a.d.n.
164-August Tham-Gablonz a.d.n.
165-Rudolf Tham-Gablonz a.d.n.
166-Camill Bergmann & Sohne-Gablonz a.d.n.
167-Augustin Hicke-Tyssa bei Bodenbach.
168-Wilhelm Fuhner-Pforzheim.
169-Paul Garthe-Milpe.
170-B.H. Mayer-Pforzheim.
171-Unknown.
172-Walter & Heniein-Gablonz a.d.n.
173-Adam Donner-Wuppertal/Elberfeld.
174-Petz & Lorenz-Unter Reichenbach.
175-Walgo-Kierspe.
176-Heinrich Vogt-Pforzheim.
177-Franz Klamt & Sohne-Gablonz a.d.n.
178-Gustav Kortel-Peterswald bei Bodenbach.
179-Unknown.
180-Metallwarenfabrik S.Jablonski-Posen.
181-Wilhelm Muller-Posen.
182-C.E.Junker-Berlin.
183-Schmahl & Schulz-Wuppertal/Barmen.
184-W.Aurich-Leipe.
185-Klein & Quencer-Idar/Oberstein.
186-Biedermann & Co-Oberkassel bei Bonn.
(Who received the last RZM number 9/1944).

Appendix C - RMZ Numbers

The German WWII RZM numbers - The German armed forces during WWII were very particular about the consistency and quality of the badges, medals, uniforms, daggers and many other items they employed. As the size of the armed forces grew so did the need for the items listed above. The need to centralize the control of quality was pressing.

This need gave birth to the Reichszeugmeisterei organization, also known as RZM. This organization was based at the Brown house in Munich and Nazi party headquarters in Berlin.

The RZM ensured that the manufacturers of military items were consistent in design, quality of materials and other characteristics of the items. It also defined standards of design, manufacturing and quality and published an authoritative color chart for textiles.

The RZM issued a number to companies so they could place it in the product they were authorized to produce. The RZM code was usually accompamied by a logo formed by the letters RZM which was contained in a circle with the letter M at the bottom.

	RZM Number	Manufacturer City
1	M7/1	Gebruder Christians,Christianswerk Solingen
2	M7/2	Emil Voos Waffenbrik Solingen
3	M7/3	Kuno Ritter Solingen-Grafrath
4	M7/4	August Muller KG Solingen-Merscheid
5	M7/5	Carl Julius Krebs Solingen
6	M7/6	H&F Lauterjung Solingen-Widdert
7	M7/7	Hermann Konejung AG, Solingen
8	M7/8	Eduard Gembruch Solingen-Grafrath
9	M7/9	Solinger Metallwarenfabrik GmBH Stoecker & Co
10	M7/10	J.A. Henckels Zwillingswerk KG Solingen
11	M7/11	E. Knecht & Co Solingen
12	M7/12	Carl Robert Kaldenbach, Waffenfabrik Max Weyersberg Solingen
13	M7/13	Artur Schuttelhofer & Co Solingen - Wald
14	M7/14	P. D. Luneschloss Solingen
15	M7/15	Carl u. Robert Linder Solingen-Weyer
16	M7/16	Justus Brenger & Co., Justinuswerk Solingen-Wald
17	M7/17	A. Werth Solingen
18	M7/18	Richard Abr. Herder Solingen
19	M7/19	Ed. Wusthof, Dreizackwerk Solingen
20	M7/20	Ernst Mandewirth Solingen
21	M7/21	Hermann Schneider Solingen
22	M7/22	Wilhelm Weltersbach Solingen
23	M7/23	Carl Halbach Solingen
24	M7/24	Reinh. Weyersberg Solingen
25	M7/25	Wilhelm Wagner Solingen-Merscheid
26	M7/h25	Jostes & Co. Solingen
27	M7/26	Jacobs & Co. , Solingen-Grafrath Carl August Meis GmBH Solingen
28	M7/27	Puma-Werk Lauterjung & Son Solingen
29	M7/28	Gustav Felix, Gloriawerk Solingen
30	M7/29	Klittermann & Moog GmBH Solingen-Haan Jacobs Jacobs & Co.
31	M7/30	Gebruder Grafrath Solingen-Widdert
32	M7/31	August Merten Ww Solingen-Grafrath
33	M7/32	Robert Muller & Sohn Solingen-Merscheid

34	M7/33	F. W. Holler	Solingen
35	M7/h33	P. u. A. Duenzer	Solingen
36	M7/34	C. Rud Jacobs	Solingen-Grafrath
37	M7/35	Wilhelm Halbach	Solingen
38	M7/36	E. u. F. Horster	Solingen
39	M7/37	Robert Klaas	Solingen-Ohligs
40	M7/38	Paul Seilheimer	Solingen
41	M7/39	Franz Steinhoff	Solingen-Wald
42	M7/40	Hartkopf & Co.	Solingen
43	M7/41	Rudolf Schmidt	Solingen
44	M7/42	WKC-Waffenfabrik GmbH [Weyersberg, Kirschbaum]	Solingen-Wald
45	M7/43	Paul Weyersberg & Co.	Solingen
46	M7/44	F.W. Backhaus GmbH	Solingen-Ohligs
47	M7/45	Karl Bocker	Solingen
48	M7/h45	Ottersbach & Co.	Solingen
49	M7/46	Emil Gierling	Solingen
50	M7/47	Paul Ebel	Solingen
51	M7/48	Otto Simon	Steinbach
52	M7/49	Friedrich Herder Abr. Sohn	Solingen
53	M7/50	Gebrüder Heller, G.m.b.H.	Marienthal
54	M7/51	Anton Wingen, Jr.	Solingen
55	M7/52	Herbertz & Meurer,	Solingen-Grafrath
56	M7/53	Nach. Gustav Weyersberg,	Solingen
57	M7/54	Gottfried Müller	Rerges-Vogtei
58	M7/55	Robert Herder	Solingen-Ohligs
59	M7/56	C. D. Schaaf	Solingen
60	M7/57	Peter Lungstrass	Solingen-Ohligs
61	M7/58	Louis Perlmann	Solingen
62	M7/59	C. Lutters & Co.	Solingen
63	M7/60	Gustav L. Koller	Solingen
64	M7/61	Carl Tillmans Sohn KG.	Solingen
65	M7/62	Friedrich Plucker Jr	Solingen-Grafrath
66	M7/63	Herder & Engels	Solingen-Ohligs
67	M7/64	Friedr. Geigis	Solingen-Foche
68	M7/65	Karl Heidelberg	Solingen
69	M7/66	Carl Eickorn	Solingen
70	M7/67	Gottlieb Hammesfahr	Solingen-Foche
71	M7/68	Tigerwerk Lauterjung & Co.	Solingen
72	M7/69	H.A. Erbe AG.	Schmalkalden
73	M7/70	David Malsch	Steinbach
74	M7/71	Herm. Hahn	Solingen-Wald
75	M7/72	Karl Rob. Kaldenbach	Solingen-Grafrath
76	M7/73	F u. A. Helbig	Steinbach
77	M7/74	Friedrich Aug. Schmitz	Solingen
78	M7/75	Böker & Co.	Solingen
79	M7/76	Herbeck & Meyer	Solingen-Weyer
80	M7/77	Gustav Schmeider	Solingen
81	M7/78	Herm. Linder Sohn	Solingen
82	M7/79	C. Bertram Reinhard & Sohn	Solingen
83	M7/80	Gustav C. Spitzer	Solingen
84	M7/81	Karl Tiegel	Riemberg
85	M7/82	Gebrüder Born	Solingen
86	M7/83	Richard Pluemacher Sohn	Solingen

87	M7/84	Carl Schmidt Sohn	Solingen
88	M7/85	Arthur Evertz	Solingen
89	M7/86	Kuno Liemscheid & Co.	Solingen auf der Hohe
90	M7/87	Malsch & Ambronn	Steinbach
91	M7/88	Juliuswerk-J. Schmidt & Sohn	Riemberg i. Schlesien
92	M7/89	Ernst Mandewirth	Solingen
93	M7/90	Eickelnberg & Mack	Solingen
94	M7/91	Carl Spitzer	Malsch
95	M7/92	Peter Daniel Krebs	Solingen
96	M7/93	Ewald Cleff	Solingen
97	M7/94	Gebrüder Bell	Solingen-Grafarth
98	M7/95	J. A. Schmidt & Sohn	Solingen
99	M7/96	Drees & Sohn	Solingen
100	M7/97	F Koeller & Co.	Solingen-Ohligs
101	M7/98	Ernst Erich Witte	Solingen
102	M7/99	Franz Weinrank	Wien
103	M7/100	Franz Pils & Sobn	Wien
104	M7/101	Fritz Weber	Wien
105	M7/102	Franz Pils & Sohn,	Steinbach am St.
106	M7/103	Josef Hack	Steyr
107	M7/104	Ludwig Zeitler	Wien
108	M7/105	Rudolf Wurzer,	St. Christophen
109	M7/106	Georg Kerschbaumer,	Steinbach an der Steyr
110	M7/107	Unknown	
111	M7/108	Karl Oschmann & Co.	Brotterode i. Th.
112	M7/109	Thomas Weilpütz	Solingen-Höscheid
113	M7/110	Felbeck & Pickard	Solingen
114	M7/111	H. Herder	Solingen
115	M7/112	Carl Wüsthof-Gladiatorwerk	Solingen
116	M7/113	Berndorfer Metaliwarenfabrik - Arthur Krupp AG.	Berndorf
117	M7/114	Hugo Linder C. W. Sohn	Solingen-Weyer
118	M7/115	Erhardt Reich	Schwcina
119	M7/116	Franz Frenzel	Nixdorf
120	M7/117	Julius Pilz Sohn	Nixdorf
121	M7/118	Jacobs & Co.	Solingen

Belt Buckle Manufactures

M4/1 through M4/47 contract code numbers were issued between March 9, 1935 and December 31, 1935

1	M4/1	Ferdinand Hofstatter Bonn a.R.
2	M4/2	Martin Winter Munchen
3	M4/3	Kallenbach, Mayer & Franke Luckenwalde
4	M4/4	Gustav Emil Ficker Beierfeld
5	M4/5	Leistner & Cie. Leipzig
6	M4/6	C. u. W. Meinel-Scholar Klingenthal
7	M4/7	Hermann Sprenger Iserlohn
8	M4/8	Rudolf Wachtler & Lange Mittweida
9	M4/9	Albert Winges Trusen (Thuringen)
10	M4/10	Bernhard Haarmann Ludenscheid
11	M4/11	August Enders AG Ludenscheid
12	M4/12	Mathias Kutsch Attendorn (MK)

13	M4/13	Paul Schuhmacher	Ludenscheid
14	M4/14	Otto Fechler	Bernsbach
15	M4/15	Paul Meybauer	Berlin SW68
16	M4/16	Robert Tummler	Döbeln
17	M4/17	Ernst Meissner	Holenlimburg
18	M4/18	Julius Bauer Söhne	Zella-Mehlis
19	M4/19	Ernst Schneider	Ludenscheid (ESL)
20	M4/20	Hillenbrand & Bröer	Ludenscheid
21	M4/21	Hans Schönfelder	Mitweide
22	M4/22	Christian Theodor Dicke	Ludenscheid (CTD; CTH)
23	M4/23	Dr. Franke & Cie KG	Ludenscheid
24	M4/24	Friedrich Linden	Ludenscheid (FLL)
25	M4/25	Noelle & Heuck KG	Ludenscheid (N&H)
26	M4/26	Offenberg-Engels	Iserlohn
27	M4/27	Overhoff & Cie	Ludenscheid (O &C; OCL)
28	M4/28	Paulmann & Crone	Ludenscheid (PC)
29	M4/29	K. Fr. Brahm	Furth
30	M4/30	Berg & Nolte AG	Ludenscheid (B&N L)
31	M4/31	Max Haufe	Grossröhrsdorf
32	M4/32	Gerbruder Hahne	Ludenscheid
33	M4/33	J.D. von Hagen GmbH	Iserlohn
34	M4/34	Heinrich Nordwall Dransfeld & Co	Menden
35	M4/35	Moeller & Schröder	Offenbach a.M.
36	M4/36	Ludenscheid Knopffabrik von Hofe & Co GmbH	Ludenscheid
37	M4/37	Stefan Merkl	Nurnberg
38	M4/38	Richard Sieper & Söhne	Ludenscheid (R.S&S.)
39	M4/39	F. W. Assmann & Söhne	Ludenscheid (A;A&S)
40	M4/40	Giesse & Schmidt	Ruhla (Thuringen)
41	M4/41	Schmal & Schultz	Wuppertal-Barmen
42	M4/42	Hermann Aurich	Dresden A16 (H.A.)
43	M4/43	H.A. Erbe	Schmalkalden
44	M4/44	Paul Cramer & Cie	Ludenscheid
45	M4/45	Cramer & Dornbach	Ludenscheid
46	M4/46	Wilhelm Schroder & Cie	Ludenscheid
47	M4/47	Ebberg & Co	Ludenscheid
48	M4/48	P.C. Turck Wwe	Ludenscheid

M4/48 through M4/64 contract code numbers were issued between January 1, 1936 and December 1936

49	M4/49	Steinhauer & Luck	Ludenscheid
50	M4/50	Willy Thuy	Ludenscheid
51	M4/51	Horner & Dittermann	Wuppertal-Barmen
52	M4/52	Linden und Funke GmbH	Iserlohn
53	M4/53	Zieh-Press-u. Stanzwerk	Zwintschona bei Halle
54	M4/54	Willy Annetsberger	Munchen
55	M4/55	Julius Kremp	Ludenscheid
56	M4/56	Friedrich Keller	Oberstein a.d. Nahe
57	M4/57	Julius Maurer	Oberstein a.d. Nahe
58	M4/58	Wilhelm Deus	Solingen
59	M4/59	Adolf Baumeister	Ludenscheid (Ad.B.L.)
60	M4/60	Gustav Brehmer	Markneukirchen (GB)
61	M4/61	Julius Dinnebier Nachf.	Ludenscheid
62	M4/62	Arld Heinrich	Nurnberg Ost
63	M4/63	Werner Redo	Saarlautern

Belt Buckles Without an RZM Number

The following manufacturers produced belt buckles, but were not licensed by the RZM

###	Manufacturer
1	Gebruder Baumgartner
2	Berkemeyer & Cie
3	Berlin SW 15
4	J. Deutschbein
5	Robert C. Dold
6	Dresden
7	Euskirchen
8	Frankfurt/Main
9	Goch/Rheinland
10	Gottlieb & Sohne
11	ARG GumbH
12	Hamburg
13	Hermann Koller
14	Konigsberg
15	Bad Kudowa I. Sch.
16	Mannheim
17	Menden
18	Josef Mold
19	Mulheim/Ruhr (B&C)
20	Nowa
21	Oberstein (L.G.S.)
22	Offenburg (RODO)
23	Pforzheim (HK)
24	L. Regensburgs
25	Schmolle & Co.
26	Springer & Co.
27	H. Tietz
28	Wiedmann

OTHER

	RZM Number	Manufacturer	City
1	M2/139	George Wetzel	Not recorded
2	M2/168	Fritz Balke	Not recorded
3	M2/169	Gebruder Tueckmantel	Not recorded
4	M2/170	E. Steineshoff & Sohne	Not recorded
5	M2/171	Gottfried Reuter	Not recorded
6	M2/172	Gebruder Knoth	Not recorded
7	M2/173	Karl Peters Jr.	Not recorded
8	M2/174	Wilhelm Otto	Not recorded
9	M2/175	Willy Goeddertz	Not recorded
10	M2/176	Rudy u. Karl Kraus	Not recorded
11	M2/177	Luettgens & Engels	Not recorded

12	M2/178	Oskar Jenish	Not recorded
13	M2/179	Peter Prass	Not recorded
14	M2/180	Karl Muller	Not recorded
15	M2/181	Bremshey & Co.	Not recorded
16	M2/182	Robert Hartmann	Not recorded
17	M2/183	Julius Kirschner & Sohn	Not recorded

OTHER

	RZM Number	Manufacturer	City
1	M/121	Troost-Wolf AG. Munchen	Not recorded
2	M/122	Josef Wolf Waffenfabrik	Not recorded
3	M/124	Karl Wolf Waffenfabrik	Not recorded
4	M/126	Wolf & Sohn (Wilhelm Wolf d. j.)	Not recorded

Appendix D
Comprehensive List of IOH Manufacturers since 1965
(Official List)

HMK	NAME	CITY / STATE
A21	ACE SCHIFFLI EMBROIDERY CO	
A22	AMERICAN INSIGNIA	
A23	ARONOFF SERVICE PRODUCTS CO	
A24	ARTISTIC WEAVING CO	POMPTON LAKES, NJ 07442
A25	ACTION EMBROIDERY CORP	ONTARIO, CA 97162
A26	AMERICAN METAL CRAFT	ATTLEBORO, MA 02703
A27	APOLLO MILITARY MANUF CO	BROOKLYN, NY 11323
A28	AMERICAN MILITARY SUPPLY CORP	
A29	AMERICAN IDENTIFICATION CO INC	
A30	ACHIEVEMENT PRODUCTS INC	EAST HANOVER, NJ 07936
A31	AMERICAN EMBROIDERY	
A32	ADRIEL BROTHERS INC	ATTLEBORO. MA 02703
A33	ACTIVE GENERATION INC	DALLAS, TX 75226
A34	ANSON INC	PROVIDENCE, RI 02907
A35	AB EMBLEMS / CONRAD INDUSTRIES	WEAVERVILLE, NC 28787
A36	AERIAL IMPRESSIONS	
A37	AWARD CRAFTERS	CHANTILLY, VA 22021
A38	ALL STATE MEDAL COMPANY INC	LODI, NJ 07644
A39	AWARDS BY WILSON TROPHY	ST LOUIS, MO 63134
A40	ALICE'S ALTERATIONS	JONESBORO, GA 10738
A41	ANTHEM INSIGNIA INC	PROVIDENCE, RI 02908
B21	L/G. BALFOUR COMPANY	ATTLEBORO, MA 02703
B22	BALLY RIBBON MILLS	BALLY, PA 19503
B23	BEE KAY PARADE EQUIPMENT CO	
B24	V.H. BLACKINGTON & CO., INC.	ATTLEBORO FALLS, MA 02763-0300
B25	BELL BRODUCTS	
B26	BENDE & SONS INC	PASSAIC, NJ 07055
B27	THE BALL & SOCKET MFG CO	CHESHIRE, CT 06410
B28	BRANDED EMBLEM COMPANY	OVERLAND PARK, KS 66204
B29	BARON	LOS ANGELES, CA 90021
B30	BS & T CORPORATION	NORTH ATTLEBORO, MA
B31	BALDWIN RIBBON & STAMPING CORP	WOODSIDE, NY 11377
B32	BD CORPORATION	
B33	B & A	MESA, AZ
B34	BROY CO MANUFACTURING & SALES CO	WEST BEND, WI 53095
B35	BROOKS AWARDS & MEDALS	ISLAND PARK, NY 11558
C21	CLOVER EMBROIDERY WORKS	
C22	CORO INC	
C23	CREST-CRAFT COMPANY	CINCINNATI, OH 45227
C24	COLUMBIA BUTTON & NAILHEAD CO	LONG ISLAND CITY, NY 11101
C25	CAROLINA SERVICE CO	
C26	CINDARN PLASTICS INC	BALTIMORE, MD 21223
C27	C&P EMBROIDERY COMPANY INC	NORTH BERGEN, NJ
C28	CAROLINA EMBLEMS COMPANY	CAMPOBELLO, SC 29322
C29	COLONIAL PROMOTIONS	
C30	COOPER INDUSTRIES	UPLAND, CA 91786

Code	Company	Location
C31	CLASSIC MEDALLICS INC	LONG ISLAND CITY, NY 11101
C32	CREATIVE MODELING & DIE MFG CO	NORTH ATTLEBORO, MA
C33	COLORADO STITCHERY	COLORADO SPRINGS, CO
C34	C&C METAL PRODUCTS	ENGLEWOOD, NJ 07631
C35	COVER STITCHES	WEST NEW YORK, NY 07093
D21	DONDERO INC	FAIRFIELD, VA 24435
D22	DENMARK'S MILITARY EQUIPMENT CORP	ASTORIA, NY 11101
D23	A.J. DENNISON CO INC	RIVERSIDE, RI 02915
D24	DELANCY SCHOOL OF MARKETING	
D25	DIVERSIFIED PRODUCTA INC	PROVIDENCE, RI 02903
D26	DETAIL MANUFACTURING CO INC	
D27	DESIGNER TOOL & DIE	SEEKONK, MA 02771
D28	DIANA'S FLAGS & GUIDONS	KILLEEN, TX 76542
D29	DISCOVERY MARKETING & DESIGN LTD	PAWTUCKET, RI 02860
D30	DIVERSIFIED METAL CRAFTERS INC.	LINCOLN, RI 02865
E21	EMBLEM & BADGE INC	PROVIDENCE, RI 02940
E22	ELCO EMBROIDERY WORKS	
E23	EMBLEM SUPPLY CO INC	
E24	EAGLE REGALIA COMPANY INC	CHESTNUT RIDGE, NY 10977
E25	EMBLEMCRAFT LTD	
E26	EVEREADY EMBROIDERY INC	JERSEY CITY, NJ 07305
E27	ERFFMEYER & SONS COMPANY INC	MILWAUKEE, WI 23223
E28	EBSCO INDUSTRIES INC	BIRMINGHAM, AL 35203
E29	ELWYN INSTITUTE	ELWYN, PA 19063
E30	EVERSON ROSS COMPANY	SPRING VALLEY, NY 10977
E31	EISEMAN-LUDMAR COMPANY INC	HICKSVILLE, NY 11801
E32	ELDEN INDUSTRIES	CRANSTON, RI 02910
E33	EAGLE CREST	JACKSONVILLE, FL 32205
E34	EMPIRE STATE METAL PRODUCTS	RICHMOND HILL, NY 11418
E35	EAGLE TOOL INC.	PROVIDENCE, RI 02909
F21N	FRIELICH BROTHERS	
F22	FULFORD MANUFACTURING COMPANY	
F23	M. FOX INC	WOODSTOCK, VT 05091
F24	FAWN INDISTRIES INC	NEW PARK, PA 17352
F25	FINISHING TOUCH EMBROIDERIES	WEST NEW YORK, NY 07093
F26	FBF INDUSTRIES INC	SOUTHHAMPTON, PA 18966
F27	BRUCE FOX INC	NEW ALBANY, IN 47151
G21	GRIP-FLEX CORPORATION	PHILADELPHIA, PA
G22	GEMSCO INC	MILFORD, CT 06460
G23	IRA GREEN INC	PROVIDENCE, RI 02905
G24	THE GREEN COMPANY INC	LENEXA, KS 66215
G25	MASTERCRAFT AWARDS AND GENERAL DISPLAY COMPANY	MANASSAS, VA 20110
G26	GREEN DUCK CORPORATION	HERNANDO, MS
G27	GRACO	TOMBALL, TX 77377-0027
G28	THE GROSS ORGANIZATION	FORT WORTH, TX 76126
G29N	SAMUAL GALLINI	NEW YORK, NY 10016
G30	GAMBER PRODUCTS COMPANY INC	WARWICK, RI 02886
G31	GREAT AMERICAN WEAVING CORP	BALLY, PA 19503
G32	GJM MANUFACTURING INC	ATTLEBORO, MA 02703
H21	JACK HELLER	
H22	THE IRVING H. HAHN COMPANY	BALTIMORE, MD 21230
H23	HARTMANN INC	

H24	HILBORN-HAMBURGER INC	PASSAIC, NJ 07055
H25	HIS LORDSHIP PRODUCTS	
H26	HIGH FLIGHT	RANCHO, CA 95670
H27	HALLMARK EMBLEM INC	TAMPA, FL 33602
H28	???	
H29	???	
H30	???	
H31N	G. HIRSCH & SONS	
H32N	MICHAEL HESSBERG	
H33	HOOK-FAST SPECIALTIES INC	PROVIDENCE, RI 02905
H34	HERNDON RECOGNITION	PORTLAND, OR 97219
I21	INTERNATIONAL INSIGNIA CORPORATION	PROVIDENCE, RI 02905
I22	IVY EMBLEMS CORPORATION	NORTH BERGEN, NJ 07093
I23	INTERSTATE LACE COMPANY	UNION CITY, NJ 07087
I24	INTER-ALL CORPORATION	GRANBY, MA 01033
J21	JOY INSIGNIA INC	DEERFIELD BEACH, FL 33441
J22	JAYMAC BOWLING SUPPLIES	ERIE, PA 16514
J23	JACQUELINE EMBROIDERY CO	TOMS RIVERS, NJ 08755
K21	KREW INCORPORATED	
K22	WILBUR C. KIFF COMPANY	
K23	E. KUGELMANN CO/GUAYNABO CORP	COLLEGE POINT, NY 11356
K25	KB SPECIALTIES	
K26	ACUTE IDEA(S)/IRA K. MEDALS	MARIETTA, GA 30068
K26	HARRY KLITZNER COMPANY INC	PROVIDENCE, RI 02907
K27	KEL-LAC UNIFORMS INC	SAN ANTONIO, TX 78227
K28	KENNEDY INCORPORATED	NORTH KINGSTOWN, RI 02852
L21	LEAVENS MANUFACTURING COMPANY	
L22	LORDSHIP INDUSTRIES INC	
L23	LEONARD CORPORATION	PHILADELPHIA, PA 19134
L24	LOMA-LINDA CHERRCO	REDLANDS, CA 92373
L25	LOUISVILLE MFG COMPANY	
L26	LION BROTHERS COMPANY INC	OWINGS MILL, MD 21117
L27	LIBERTY INSIGNIA CORPORATION	AMHERST, NY 14226
L28	LEARY'S MILITARY COMPANY	WILMINGTON, DE 19805
L29	LETTERS MEDALS INCORPORATED	SAN JUAN, PR 00902
M21	MILITARY POST SUPPLIERS	
M22	N.S. MEYER INCORPORATED	
M23	McCABE BROTHERS	NEW YORK, NY 10038
M24	MILITARY MANUFACTURERS OF MD	
M25	???	
M26	MERIT RIBBON COMPANY	
M27	LOREN MURCHISON COMPANY	
M28	MINERO-NEWCOMBE COMPANY	
M29	MIDWEST TROPHY COMPANY	DEL CITY, OK 73115
M30	MAGIC NOVELTY COMPANY INC	NEW YORK, NY 10034
M31N	S. MARS	
M32N	MILITARY EQUIPMENT CORPORATION	MORRISTOWN, NJ 07960
M33	THE METALCRAFT MINT INC	GREEN BAY, WI 54303
M34	ADVANTAGE EMBLEM INC	DULUTH, MN 55808
M35	McALLISTER INDUSTRIES INC	
M36	MOTEX INCORPORATED	WEST NEW YORK, NY 07093
M37	MEDALS OF AMERICA	FOUNTAIN INN, SC 29644
M38	MAACS INCORPORATED	WELLS, ME 04090

M39	MIL-BAR PLASTICS INC.	CORONA, CA 92879
N21	NATIONAL EMBLEM & EMBROIDERY	
N22	NEW ENGLAND TROPHY & ENGRAVING	
N23N	KEN NOLAN INCORPORATED	IRVINE, CA 92713
N24N	NEWTEL INCORPORATED	MIAMI, FL 33135
N25	C.W. NIELSON MFG CORPORATION	CHEHALIS, WA 98532
N26	NORTHEAST EMBLEM & BADGE	CHESHIRE, CT 06410
N27	NATIONAL EMBLEM INCORPORATED	CARSON, CA 90746
N28	NATIONAL DIE & BUTTON MOLD	CARLSTADT, NJ 07072
N29	NELLIE'S ALTERATION & MANUF	MOUNTAIN BROOK, AL 35223
N30	THE NORTH ATTLEBORO JEWELRY CO	ATTLEBORO, MA 02703
N31	NORTHWEST TERRITORY MINT	AUBURN, WA 98001
N40N	Number N40N through N61N were given to the US Navy for their use.	
N41N		
N42N		
N43N		
N44N		
N45N		
N46N		
N47N		
N48N		
N49N		
N50N	These numbers have been assigned to the U.S. Navy	
N51N		
N52N		
N53N		
N54N		
N55N		
N56N		
N57N		
N58N		
N59N		
N60N		
N61N		
O21	ORBER MANUFACTURING COMPANY	GARDEN CITY, RI 02920
O22	OFFICER'S EQUIPMENT COMPANY	STAFFORD, VA 22554
O23	OLYMPIC TROPHY & AWARDS CO	CHICAGO, IL 60639
O24	THE OAK BASKET	LAUREL, MS 39440
O25	RS OWENS & COMPANY	CHICAGO, IL 60630
P21	POLK SALES COMPANY	
P22	PREFAX INCORPORATED	
P23	EP INDUSTRIES INCORPORATED	
P24	ED PEREIRA INCORPORATED	
P25	PECAS EMBROIDERY CORPORATION	NORTH BERGEN, NJ 04047
P26	PERSONALLY YOURS	WENATCHEE, WA 98801
P27	PENN EMBLEM COMPANY	PHILADELPHIA, PA 19154
P28	PEERLESS EMBROIDERY COMPANY	CHICAGO, IL 60618
P29	PATRIOT INSIGNIA	BOHEMIA, NY 11716
P30	PIECES OF HISTORY	CAVE VREEK, AZ 85327
P31	PARAMOUNT MANUFACTURING CO	GREENVILLE, RI 02828
P32	PATRIOT IDENTITY	SANBORN, NY 14132
R21	THE ROBBINS COMPNAY	ATTLEBORO, MA 02703
R22	D.J. RYAN INCORPORATED	

R23	THE REGAL EMBLEM COMPANY INC	NEW YORK, NY 10013
R24	THE REYNOLDS COMPANY	
R25	RAINBOW EMBLEMS	
R26	RAY INCORPORATED	HOUDTON, TX 77091
R27	RAINBOW EMBROIDERY	EAST BRUNSWICK, NJ 08816
R28	ROCKY MOUNTAIN MEMORABILIA	ALAMOSA, CO 81101
R29	RIVER CITY PATTERN INC	CLACKAMAS, OR 97015
R30	RELIABLE WORLD TRADE COMPANY INC	OAKLAND, CA 94603
R31	REGIMENTAL SIGN COMPANY	WASHINGTON, DC 20012
S21	HARRY SUGERMAN INCORPORATED	
S22	SILVERMAN CORPORATION	
S23	STANDARD MANUFACTURING CO	
S24	SHERMAN MANUFACTURING CO	
S25	SNAG-PRUFE FASTENERS	LOUISVILLE, KY 40233-6351
S26	SUPREME MILITARY INSIGNIA	
S27	SCHIFFLI CORPORATION OF AMERICA	
S28	SHALHOUB BROTHERS	BAYONNE, NJ 07002
S29	SWISS-TEX CORPORATION	
S30	BEN SILVER COMPANY	
S31	N.G. SLATER CORPORATION	NEW YORK, NY 10011
S32	SWISSARTEX EMBLEM INC	ASHVILLE, NC 28814-0239
S33	SCHREYER EMBROIDERY COMPANY	FAIRVIEW, NJ 07022
S34	STAY SHARP TOOL COMPANY INC	NORTH ATTLEBORO, MA
S35	SIMBA AWARDS	
S36	STRANGE COMPANY	
S37	SUTTON MANUFACTURING	EAST PROVIDENCE, RI 02914
S38	THE SUPPLY ROOM	OXFORD, AL 36203
S39	STA-BRIGHT PRODUCTS	BALTIMORE, MD 21211
S40	SWISS MAID INCORPORATED	GREENTOWN, PA 18426
S41	SCHWEIZER EMBLEM COMPANY	PARK RIDGE, IL 60068
S42	STADRI EMBLEMS INC	WOODSTOCK, NY
S43	WM. J. SIRAVO DESIGNS INC	CRANSTON, RI 02921
S44	SAYRE ENTERPRISES	BUENA VISTA, VA 24416
S45	SPORTS CADDY I LLC	CHARLOTTE, NC 28217
S46	SUPERIOR DIE & STAMPING INC	NORTON, MA 02766
S47	SUN BADGE COMPANY	SAN DIMAS, CA 91773
S48	STITCH GALLERY INC	HARLINGEN, TX 78550
S49	STITCHIN POST	BRADENTON, FL 34208
S50	SMITH & WARREN	WHITE PLAINS, NY 10601
S51	SMART DESIGN INC.	WOODBRIDGE, VA 22191
T21	INTERNATIONAL ENTERPRISES LTD	PROVIDENCE, RI 02909
T22	TC ART & CRAFT WORKS	HONOLULU, HI 96825
T23	A&S TAUB	BELLEVIEW, WA 98009
T24	TOMMY TUCKER T-SHIRTS	TUCSON, AZ 85713
T25	TELEPUNCH INCORPORATED	PALATINE, IL 60067
U21	URSCHEL TOOL CORPORATION	CRANSTON, RI 02907
U22	UNITED UNIFORM ACCESSPRIES INC	LONG ISLAND CITY, NY 11101
U23	UNIVERSAL SPECIALTY AWARDS INC	PAWTUCKET, RI 02860
V21	VANGUARD MILITARY EQUIPMENT CORP (EAST)	NORFOLK, VA 23502
V21	VANGUARD MILITARY EQUIPMENT CORP (WEST)	CARLSBAD, CA 92008
V22	VOYAGER EMBLEMS	SANBORN, NY 14132
W21	WATERBURY COMPANIES INC	WATERBURY, CT 06702
W22	WOLF-BROWN INCORPORATED	

W23	WESTERN MILITARY SUPPLY COMPANY	
W24	WARNER WOVEN LABEL COMPANY INC	PATERSON, NJ 07504
W25	WILLIAMS & ANDERSON COMPANY	CRANSTON, RI 02920
W26	WICK EMBROIDERY COMPANY	UNION CITY, NJ 07087
W27	WILLIAMS & SONS	
W28	WIL-TEX INDUSTRIES	PATERSON, NJ 07503
W29	WINDSOR GRAMERCY CORPORATION	NEW YORK, NY 10018
W30	WARWICK EMBLEM SUPPLY	WARWICK, RI 02886
W31	WENDWLL'S INCORPORATED	RAMEY, MN 55303
W32	WEINGARTEN GALLERY	FISHERS, IN 46040
Y21	YORKTOWNE SPORTS INCORPORATED	COCKEYSVILLE, MD 21030
Z21	ZART'S INCORPORATED	PAWTUCKET, RI 02860

INDEX

Title	Page number
1920 s- 1930 s Clutches	6
5B	59
6W	222
A. Valcan	207
A.F. Apple Co	37
A.H. Dondero	75
A.J. Dennison, Riverside, RI.	71
A.J. Hawkins I	104
A&S Taub	199
AB Emblems	28
Ace Novelty	28
Ace Schiffli Embroidery Co.	28
Achievement Products, Inc.	29
Action Embroidery Corp	29, 168
Active Generation	29
Adriel Brothers, Inc.	29
Advantage Emblem Inc.	30
AEco	32
Aerial Impressions	30
Alberti & Co.	30
Alice s Alterations	30
All State Medal Co. Inc.	31
Allen Uniform Company	31
Alois Rettenmaier GmbH und Co. KG	168
Alvin H. Hankins	102
Amcraft	31
American Emblem, Utica, NY	32
American Embroidery	32
American Identification Products	32
American Insignia Co, NY	33
American Metal Crafts Co	31
American Military Supply Corp.	34
American Mint	138
Amico	33
AMS	34
Anataya Brothers, Inc.	34
Andrew Butler Insignia	156
Angelo Di Maria, Inc.	69, 73
Angus & Coote	35
Anson Inc.	35
Anthem Insignia Inc.	36
Aoki Metals	36
Apollo Jewelry Mfg. Co.	36
Appendix A	224
Appendix B	227
Appendix C	229
Appendix D	235
Aresta	37
Army-Navy Equipment Co	38
Aronoff Service Products Co.	38
Arthur Johnson Manufacturing Co	118
Arthus Bertrand	49
Assmann & Sohne	38
Associate Military Stores	38
AT Gunner & Co.	100
Augis	39
August C. Frank Co.	88
Award Crafters, Inc.	40
Awards by Wilson Trophy	40
B & A	43
B. A. Ballou & Co. Inc.	43
B. Hecker	104
B.J. Co.	53
B&U Co.	44
Bailey, Banks & Biddle	40
Baldwin Ribbon & Stamping	41
Bally Ribbon Mills	43
Barnet Ludski & Son	132
Bastian Brothers (B.B.Co.). I, M	44
Bates & Klinke, Inc.	45
Bauring Jewelers	46
BD Corp	43
Bee-Kay Parade Equipment Co.	47
Bell & Brinkner	47
Bell Trading Post	47
Ben Silver, Inc.	184
Bende & Sons Inc	48
Berben Insignia Co.	49
Best Emblem Company	70
Best Embroidery Company	70
Beverly Craft.	50
Biederman Co.	52
Bijou	52
Bippart, Griscomb and Osborn	53
Black, Starr & Frost, Ltd	54
Blumberg Bros	55
Bond	55
Branded Emblem Co.	56
Braxmar N.Y.	56
Brooks Awards & Medals	58
Broy Co Mfg & Sales Co	58
Bruce Fox Inc.	86
BS & T CORPORATION	58
Buerge	58
C & P EMBROIDERY CO, INC	59
C. B. Dyer	79
C. E. Hayward Company	102
C. Pacagnini	158
C. Ridabock & Co.	171

Name	Page
C.A. Winship	219
C.Balmberger	43
C.H. Wallbank Company	212
C&C Metal Products	59
CAPA	59
Carl Hirsch & Sons Iron and Rail Co.	110
Carl Poellath	163
Carolina Emblems Co	61
Carolina Service Co.	61
Cartier	60
Charles Polk CP	165
Charles R. Robbins Company	173
Cindarn Plastics Inc	61
Citco	61
CKS	62
Classic Medallics, INc	62
Clayton	63
Clover Embroidery Works	63
Clutches 1920's - 1903's	
Cohn & Rosenberger	64
College Shops	63
Colonial Promotions	63
Colorado Stitchery	63
Columbia Button & Nailhead Corp.	63
Conrad Inds.	28
Cooper Industries	64
Coro	64
Cover Stitches	65
Craftens Inc.	65
Creative Modeling & Die Mfg Co.	65
Creed Jewelry	65
Crest-Craft Co.	66
Crisalli	66
Crispulo Zamora	223
D. George Collins, Ltd.	64
D. L. Auld Company	39
D.J. Ryan Inc	176
Dallas Cap & Emblem Mfg., Inc.	29
Dan S. Dunham	78
Danecraft, Inc.	67
Daniel Low & Co.	67
Daniel Smilo & Sons	187
Dating US Insignia	3
Davidson& Sons Jewelry Company Inc.	69
Davorn Industries	69
DAWN - McCarthy & Hamrick	69
Delancy School of Marketing	70
Denazio	70
Denmark s Military Equipment Corp.	70
Deschler & Sohn	71
Designer Tool & Die	72
Detail Manufacturing Co Inc.	72
Diana s Flags & Guidons	72
Dibb Jewelers	73
Dieges & Clust	73
Discovery Marketing & Design	73
Diversified Metal Crafters Inc.	73
Diversified Products Inc.	73
Dobbins.	74
Dodge & Asher	74
Dodge Inc.	74
Dodge Trophy Co.	74
Dohmer	75
Dommers	75
Donner	76
Dorest Company	76
Dorst Jewelry and Mfg. Co	76
DRAGO	77
Durocharm	78
E & H Simon Inc.	185
E. A. Dreher & Son	77
E. P. Industries	161
Eagle Regalia Co.	79
Eagle Tool Inc.	79
Ebsco Industries, Inc.	80, 144, 211
Ed Pereia Inc.	161
Edgar F Baton	42
Eiseman-Ludmar Co, Inc.	80
Eisenstadt Jewelry Co.	81
Eisenstadt Manufacturing Co.	81
Elco Embroidery Works	82
Elden Industries	82
Eli Hertzberg Jewelry Company	107
Elwyn Industries Inc.	82
Emblem and Badge Co.	82
Emblem Supply Co. Inc.	83
Emblematic Trades, Inc.	83
Emblemcraft Ltd	82
Empire State Metal Products	83
Erffmeyer & Son, Inc.	83
Esco	83
Eveready Embroidery Inc.	84
Everson Ross Co.	84
F. H. Noble & Co.	151
F.A. Aquino	37
F.M. Wickham	218
Fawn Industries Inc.	84
FBF Industries Inc.	84
Finishing Touch Embroideries	85
Firmin & Sons	85
FIX	85

Name	Page
Fontana Rehabilitation Workshop	86
Fox Military Equipment Co.	87
Frank Brothers	88
Franz Sturies	194
Freeman Daughaday Co	69
Frielich Brothers	88
Fritz Buttner & Sohn	58
FROM OFFICAL DIE	205
Fulford Mfg. Co.	90
G & T Young	222
G. B. Rota	175
G. Bregonzio	57
G. Hirsch & Sons	111
G.C.Meyer Company	139
Gamber Products Co. Inc.	90
Gemsco	91
General Display Co.	92
General Embroidery and Military Supply Company	91
General Insignia Corp.	93
General Products	93
General Products Company, Inc.	93
George & Sidney s Brass Shop	94
George Alan Co	30
George S. Gethen Co.	94
Gerocastelli	94
GGFXA	95
GIBCO	95
GJM Mfg. Inc.	95
Gleason-Wallace	95
Goodwear Fabrics	95
Gordon B. Miller & Co.	96
Gordon s Fort Meade	96, 143
Graco Awards, Inc.	96, 153
Grannat Brothers	97
Great American Weaving Corp	97
Guérault	99
Gus Manufacturing Co.	100
Gustav Brehmer	57
Gustave Fox Co.	86
H F Wichman & Co.	218
H. F. Linder Co.	128
H. H. P. Whittemore and Co	217
H.E. Heacock Co.	104
Hallmark Emblems Inc	101
Hallmarking	VI
Haltom Jewelers	101
Harding	103
Harding Uniform & Regalia Co	103
Harry Klitzner Co., Inc.	122
Harry R Newcome & Co.	149
Harry Sugerman Company	195
Hartegen	103
Hartmann Inc.	103
Havens & Co	103
Heckethorn Mfg. & Supply Co.	104
The Hefter-Reib Co.	105
Herdon Recognition	107
Hess & Albertson	108
Hickok Manufacturing Co.	107
High Flight	110
Hilborn & Hamburger, Inc	108
History	1
HLI Lordship Industries, Inc.	111, 130
Homrichous	112
Huguenin Freres & Co	112
Hullin	113
Humrichous Co	112
Imperial Insignia Manufacturing Company	113
INDEX	241
Industrial Support Systems	86
Insignia Co of America	113
Insignia Pin Backs & Clutches	5
International Insignia Corp	114
Interstate Lace Co.	114
IoH List of Concerns Authorized to Manufacturer Military Insignia	18
Ira Greene Co	99, 144
Iron & Russell	115
Irvin H. Hahn Company	101
Irvine & Jachens	115
J. A. Meyers & Co.	142
J. Ando	36
J. Balme	44, 162
J. J. Sweeney Jewelry Co.	196
J. Milton	145
J. O. Pollack Co.	165
J. O Brian Badge Company	154
J. R. Wood Products Corp.	220
J. W. Richardson & Co.	170
J.B.Caco	59
J.M. Schriade	118, 178, 180
J.R. Gaunt & Son	90
Jack Heller	105
Jacqueline Embroidery Co.	116
Jaurez	116
Jaymac Bowling Supplies	116
Jeannot - Beaune	46
Jenkel Jewelers	116
Jennot Beanne	46
Jerry Massey	135
Jessop Jeweler	117
Jewell Harding & Co	103
JMS Jewelry Co	118, 178, 180

Joe C. Bettencourt Company	50
John Frick Jewelry Co.	89
Johnson 1836 srl	119
Johnson National	120
Joseph Mayer	136
Joseph Mayr	136
Jostens, Inc.	117
Joy Insignia Inc	120
K. B. Specialties	121
K. G. Luke Co.	133
Kalka Maschinenstickerei GbR	120
Karl J. Klein	123
Katzson Brothers	121
Kel-lac Uniforms Inc.	121
Ken Nolan Inc.	152
Kennedy Inc	121
Klammer	122
Konwal	123, 215
Krew, Inc.	123
Kyoto	124
L. Christian Lauer	125
L.G. Balfour	41
Laorer	124
Leary s Military Company	125
Leavens Awards	126
Leavens Manufacturing Co.	126
Leonard Embroidery Company	126
Letters Medals Inc.	127
LeVelle & Co.	127
Liberty Emblem Co.	127
Linz Brothers Jewelers	130
Lord and Taylor	130
Lordship Industries, Inc.	111, 130
Loren Murchison & Co.	147
Lorioli Castelli	94
Lorioli Fratelli	89
Los Angeles Rubber Stamp Co.	131
Louis Stern Co.	193
Louisville Mfg. Co.	132
Ludlow & Co.	132
Luxenberg	133, 214
M. Fred Hirsch Co.	110
M.M. Graham	97
M.S. Bowman	56
Maco-Boch	134
Magic Novelty Co. Inc	134
Marlow White Co.	134
Marples and Beasley	135
Marshall Field & Company	135
Marshall Field s	135
Martin Kahn	120
MasterCraft Awards	92
McCabe Brothers	136
Medallic Art Co.	137, 153
Medals of America	137
Merit Ribbon Co.	138
Mermod, Jaccard & King	138
Metal Arts Co.	138
Metal Quality Marks	11
Michael Hessberg, Inc.	108
Midwest Trophy Co.	142
Mil-Bar Plastic Inc	143
Military Art & Emblem Co.	143
Military Equipment Corp.	143
Military Hallmark Coding	15
Military Manufacturers of Maryland	96, 143
Military Post Suppliers	143
Military Service Company	144, 153, 211
Miller Jewelry Company	96
Minero-Newcome Co	145
Minister	145
Monarch Military Products Co., Inc.	146
Moody Bros.	146
Morgan s	146
Motex Inc.	146
Mourgeon	146
MTM Recognition	142
N. R. Newcome & Co.	150
N.B.I.	148
N.C. Dorrety	76
N.G. Slater Corp.	187
N.S. Meyer	139
Nanco	147
National Badge & Insignia Co.	147
National Decoration Co.	148
National Die & Button Mold	148
National Guard Equipment Company	148
Nellie s Alteration & Mfg.	148
Nelson Company	149
New England Trophy & Engraving Co	150
Newtel, Inc.	150
Niderost & Taber	151
Norsid Mfg	152
Northeast Emblem & Badge	153
Northern Mint	153
Northern Stamping Co	153
Northwest Territory Mint	153
Nudelman Bros.	154
O.C. Tanner Company	198
Officers Equipment Co	155, 156
Old Badge Club	156
Olympic Trophy & Awards Co.	156
Oppenstein Brothers Jewelers	157
Orber Manufacturing Co.	157

Other Silver Hallmarks by County / Region 13

P.J. Friedel	87
Pancraft	158
Paramount Jewelers	158
Parry & Parry	158
Pasquale Uniform Company	159
Patriot Identity	159
Patriot Insignia	160
Pauls	160
Paye & Baker Mfg. Co	160
Pecas Embroidery Corp.	160
Peerless Embroidery Co.	160
Penn Emblem Co.	161
Personally Yours	161
Philadelphia Badge Co.	162
Phillips Publications	162
Pichelklammer	163
Pichiani-Barlacci	163
Pichlklammer	163
Pieces of History	163
Polar Flight.	164
Preface	V
Prefax Inc.	166
Preisser	166
Princeton Industries, Inc.	166
R. F. Simmons Co.	186
R. Liebmann Manufacturing Company	128
R.K. & Co.	172
Rainbow Emblems, Inc.	166
Rainbow Embroidery	166
Ray Incorporated	166
Reed & Barton Silversmiths	166
Regal Emblem Co.	167
Regimental Sign Co.	167
Reliable World Trade Co., Inc	168
Rentz Brothers	168
Rex Products Corp	169
Ricci, Firenze	170
Rixtine	172
Robbins Co.	173
Rock Island Arsenal	174, 205
Rocky Mountain Memorabila	174
Roland	174
Rosenfield Uniform Co	175
Russell Uniform Co.	176
S. Mars, Inc	135
S.D. Childs & Co.	61
S.E. Eby	80
Samual Gallini	90
Sayre Enterprises	177
Schreyer Embroidery Co.	177
Schweizer Emblem Co.	179
Schwertner & Cie	178
Sendai	179
Shalhoub Brothers	180
Shanholtz Joseph M Jeweler	118, 178, 180
Sheridan	181
Sherman Manufacturing Co.	182
Sherve, Treat & Eacret	183
Shreve & Co.	182
Shuttles Bros & Lewis, Inc.	183
Silverman Brothers	184
Silverman Corp	184
Simba Awards, Ltd.	184
Simco	185
Simon and Sons, Ltd	186
Simon Brothers	187
Smart Design Inc	188
Smith And Warren	189
Snag-Prufe Fasteners	189
Spies Brothers, Inc.	189
Spink and Son Ltd.	190
Sports Caddy LLC	190
SS Ltd	186
Sta-Bright Products	191
Stabilimenti Artistici	190
Stadri Emblems Inc.	191
Standard Manufacturing Co	191
Starcrest	191
Stay Sharp Tool Co. Inc.	192
Stefano Johnson	192
Stempel-Schutz	193
Stitch Gallery Inc.	193
Stitchen Post	194
Stokes & Sons	194
Sugerman	195
Sun Badge Co.	195
Superior Die & Stamping Inc.	195
Supreme Military Insignia	195
Susco	195
Sussman	196
Sutton Mfg	196
Swank, Inc.	196
Swift & Fisher	198
Swiss Maid Inc.	197
Swiss-Tex Corp.	198
T&P.	199
Taxco	199
TC Art & Craft Works	199
Teh Ling	200
Telepunch Inc.	199
The Ball & Socket Mfg. Co.	42
The Dawson Company	70
The Green Company	98
The Greenduck Corp.	97

Entry	Page
The Gross Organization	99
The Henderson-Ames Co.	106
The Kinney Co.	122
The M. C. Lilly Co.	128
The Metalcraft Mint Inc.	138
The Naval Uniform Service	149
The North Attleboro Jewelry Co.	153
The Oak Basket	154
The Reynolds Co.	169
The Roulet Company	175
The Rowland Company	176
The Supply Room, Inc.	196
The Wallace Co., Inc.	212
Theo Meyer Badgemaker	142
Thomas Co.	200
Thomas Fattorini, Ltd	200
Thomas Frattorinin	89
Thomas Stokes & Sons	194
Tiffany & Co. Inc.	201
Tommy Tucker T-Shirts	202
Tru Art Jewelry Co., In	203
Truart	203
Tucker Shean	203
U.S. Infantry Association	207
U.S. Specialty Co.	207
Uncas Manufacturing Company, Inc	204
United Emblem Co.	204
United Insignia Company Inc.	205
United Military	205
United States Government	205
United Uniform Accessories Inc.	206
Universal Specialty Awards	206
Uris Sales Corp	206
Urschel Tool Corp.	207
US Military Hallmarks	15
US Mint	205
USMC Quartermaster Insignia Serial Numbers (Certification)	17
V. H. Blackinton Company	54
V. Haacke & Co.	100
V. Saracino	177
Van Wormer & Rodrigues	209
Vanalen Company	207
Vanguard Insignia Co.	208
Vanguard Military Equip. Co	208
Vargas Manufacturing Company	209
Vintage Jewelry ID by Pin Findings	4
Volupte, Inc.	210
Voyager Emblems	210
Vulcan	211
Vulcan Industries	211
W. A. Valdez	207
W. H. Horstmann & Sons	111
W. Lutz	133
W. R. Richards	171
Wall & Dougherty	211
Wallace Bishop Co.	53
Wallace Bishop Co.	211
Wallenstein	212
Walter Dibb & Sons	73
Walter E. Hayward Company, Inc.	102
Walter Lampl Co	124
Warner Woven Label Company Inc	212
Warren Jay Products Corp.	116
Warwick Emblem Supply	213
Waterbury Companies, Inc.	213
Wehing Brothers Mfg.	213
Weidmann	213
Weingarten Gallery	133, 214
Wellington	214
Wendell & Co.	215
Wendwll s Inc.	215
Western Military Supply Co	215
Weyersberg, Kirschbaum & Co	222
Weyhing Brothers Manufacturing Company	213, 216
Whitehead and Hoag	216
Wick Embroidery Co	218
Wil-Tex Industries	218
Wilbur C. Kiff Co.	122
Wilhelm Helding	106
William Link & Co	129
William Scully Ltd.	179
Williams & Anderson, Co.	218
Windsor Gramercy Corp.	219
Wm. J. Siravo Designs Inc.	187
Wolf Appleton Co.	220
Wolf-Brown, Inc.	220
World Merchandise Co	221
World War II	7
Wright and Street	221
Yorktowne Sports Inc.	222
Young & Co.	222
Zart s Inc.	223

Made in the USA
San Bernardino, CA
13 January 2016